The Art of Cor Anglais

by

Geoffrey Browne

Who needs this book?

- Cor anglais players who cannot gain access to specialist teaching.

- Oboe players doing cor anglais auditions.

- Oboe players who have inadvertently landed a cor anglais job.

- Students who have taken up cor anglais to get out of second study piano.

- Woodwind teachers who want to keep ahead.

- Recording Engineers.

- Composers and Conductors.

- Anyone who wants to know about the concept of playing the cor anglais.

Published in London by

Sycamore Publishing

Introduction

What makes the cor anglais different from the oboe? One statement can almost suffice. It is the ORCHESTRAL REPERTOIRE. Cor anglais tunes are often much longer and lonelier than those written for the oboe and the big cor anglais solos do not appear so frequently, so perhaps it takes longer to learn to be a cor anglais player. There are other differences. The air pressure is often lower, the *vibrato* slower, the embouchure is different in that you do not play so far down the reed as on an oboe, and the sound of the instrument inspires composers to write solos quite different in style and feeling to music they write for the oboe. So, if you know the oboe repertoire then you do not necessarily have much insight into the repertoire for cor anglais, and vice versa.

For anyone attempting to play co-principal oboe in addition to cor anglais, the main difficulties are firstly of knowing the entire orchestral repertoire twice over and secondly of trying to play two instruments just as well as somebody who specialises in only one.

I have designed this book to interest as wide a range of people as possible and I have tried to cram as much information as I could into the smallest practicable space. Maybe teachers will find some ideas they can adapt for other instruments. Perhaps a recording engineer will be interested in my ideas on acoustics. Conductors have sometimes thought cor anglais players to be unfathomable creatures and perhaps this book will do something to put this right. What I have tried to do is to provide a useful collection of extracts and a summary of my method of teaching. Some of the pieces which look the easiest on paper can be quite difficult in practice, while some of the longer solos, which people often fear, can be made quite comfortable with a little expertise.

As a student, I had worked as a music copyist for Boosey & Hawkes. Before 1967, when I first joined a symphony orchestra, I was a musician working in the theatres, playing woodwind and percussion. For a short time, I was also the harpsichord tuner at the Aldwych Theatre in London. My time with the Royal Shakespeare Company was a fantastic education. I used to attend all the rehearsals that were open to me and to talk with many actors about the plays and the actor's craft. Memories of scenes from *Hamlet, Twelfth Night*, the *Henrys*, and *Shrew*, remain with me to this very day. There were parts of *The Revengers' Tragedy* I used to watch from the wings at every performance. However, one of the strongest influences in my musical development was Nadia Boulanger who gave masterclasses at the Royal College of Music in London, and who later conducted the BBC Symphony Orchestra when I was a member.

As a child, I had wanted to be an actor and then a singer. I could do neither of these things, but in learning to play a musical instrument I found both a voice and a stage. Thus, in this book, you will find not only technical tips on how to tackle the quoted extracts, but also ideas on the drama I find in the music. It is not my intention to tell you "this is how it must be done" but to give you a basis on which to form your own ideas. I hope this will be of particular use to people who live in remote areas or those who do not have access to specialist teaching.

Note

The pieces have been roughly grouped so that each double page presents similar challenges. For instance, if you are going to practise Shostakovich 8th, you might as well also practise *Ein Heldenleben,* so these appear together. The extracts are listed in alphabetical order in the Table of Contents.

I have given metronome marks for each extract as a very approximate guide. Where they are in brackets they are my own inventions, and where they are not in brackets the metronome marks have been taken from the printed score. All the cor anglais parts are transposed as normal (in F) except where marked. References to notes you play are to the fingered notes, except where they are stated to be at concert pitch. Cues are at concert pitch.

Note to second edition. Six extracts have been added, with text. Some existing extracts have been extended. The book has been revised and reorganised, and now covers the exam requirements for the Royal Academy of Music in London.   G. B. 2000.

Text © Copyright Geoffrey Browne 1996 and 2000

ISBN   0 9527300 1 4

CONTENTS

		Music	Text
Berlioz	La Damnation de Faust	15	39
Berlioz	Symphonie Fantastique	12	38
Berlioz	Rob Roy Overture	14	39
Berlioz	Roman Carnival	24	41
Britten	Nocturne	32	44
Debussy	La Mer	25	42
Debussy	Three Nocturnes	20	41
Dvořák	New World Symphony (No.9)	19	40
de Falla	The Three Cornered Hat	29	44
Franck	Symphony in D minor	15	39
Mahler	Rückert Lieder	26	43
Mahler	Kindertotenlieder	27	43
Rachmaninov	The Bells	31	44
Ravel	Piano Concerto in G major	9	37
Ravel	Rapsodie Espagnole	30	44
Respighi	The Pines of Rome	10	37
Rodrigo	Guitar Concerto	23	41
Rossini	William Tell	11	38
Shostakovich	8th Symphony	7	36
Shostakovich	10th Symphony	8	37
Sibelius	The Swan of Tuonela	2	34
Strauss, R.	Ein Heldenleben	6	35
Stravinsky	The Rite of Spring	28	43
Tchaikovsky	Romeo and Juliet	18	40
Tchaikovsky	The Nutcracker	29	43
Verdi	A Masked Ball	17	40
Verdi	The Willow Song from Otello	16	40
Wagner	Tristan Act III	4	34
Reeds			33
The Sling			33
Circular Breathing	how to do it		45
Historical Notes			45
Notes for Composers			46
Middle D, A-flat / Low E, E-flat, D / Low B flat			47
Water in the Octave Key			47
Intonation			47
Acoustics and Recording			49
The Performing Artist			50
No Air on the A string	developing the concept		50
Postscript			51
Acknowledgements			inside back cover

The Swan of Tuonela

Text p. 34

Jean Sibelius
1865 - 1957

Corno Inglese (Solo)

© Breitkopf & Härtel, Wiesbaden

Tristan und Isolde
Act III

Text p. 34

Richard Wagner
1813 - 1883

Englisches Horn (Solo)

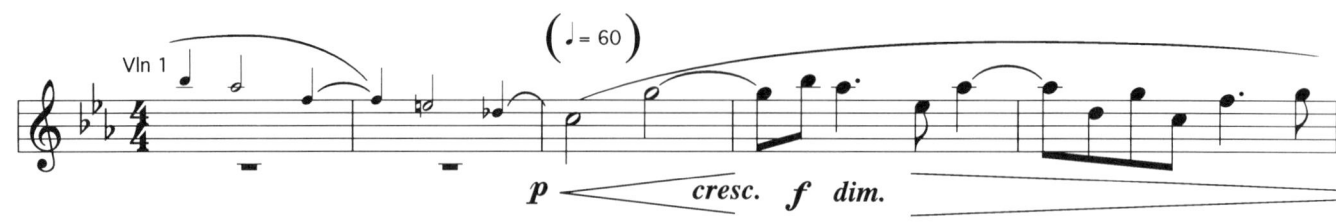

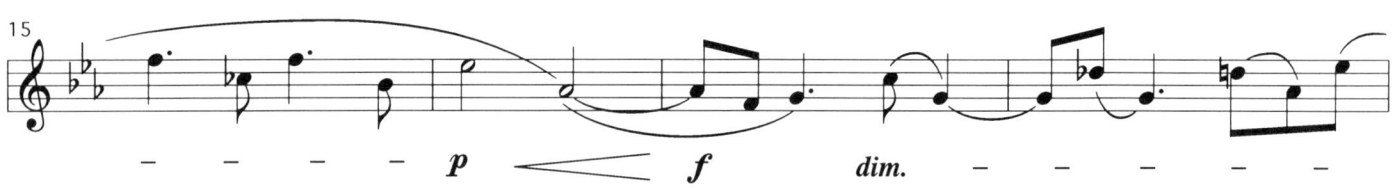
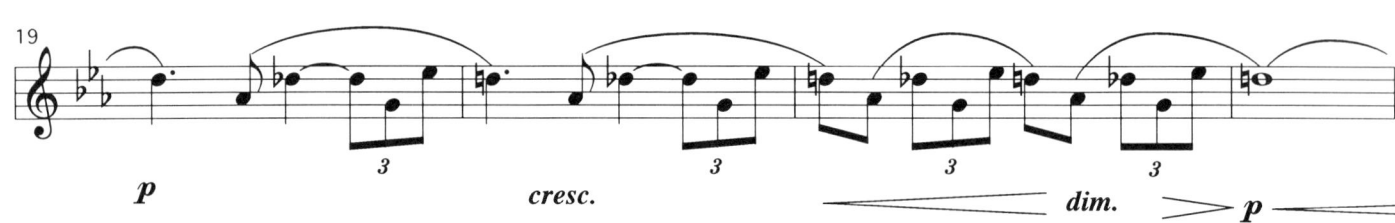
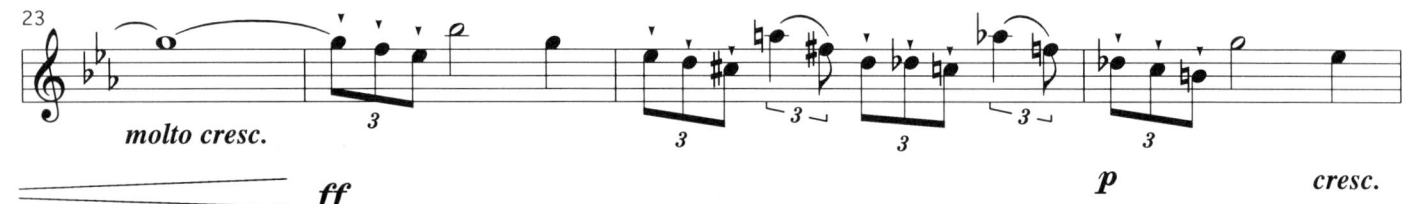

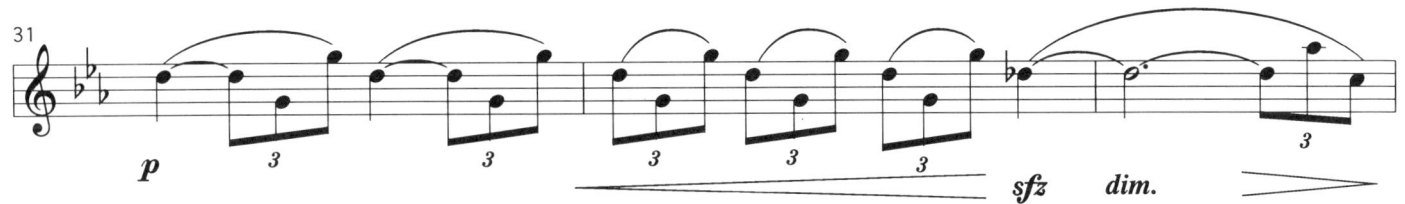
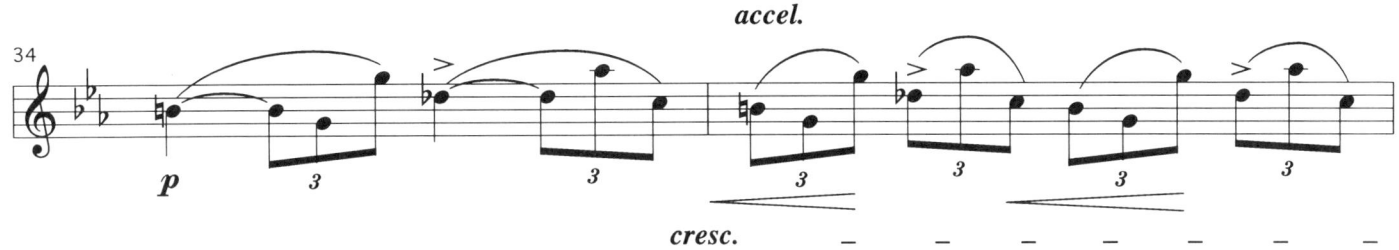
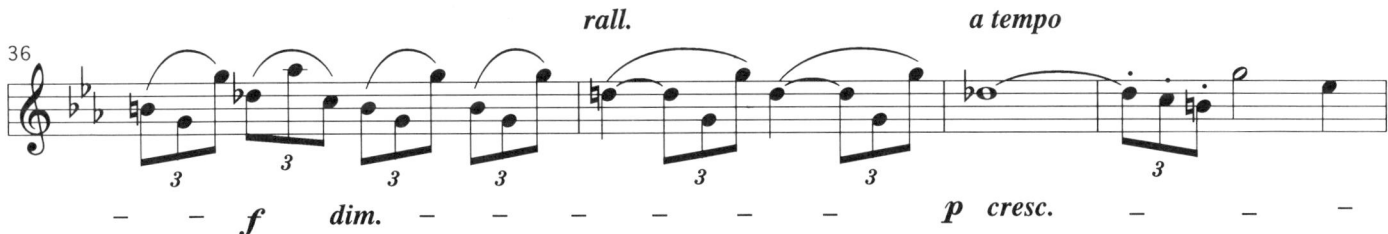

Ein Heldenleben

Text p. 35

Richard Strauss
1864 - 1949

Reprinted by permission of F.E.C. Leuckart, Munich

Symphony No. 8

Text p. 36

Dmitri Shostakovich
1906 - 1975

Symphony No. 10

Text p. 37

Dmitri Shostakovich
1906 - 1975

Piano Concerto in G Major

Text p. 37

Maurice Ravel
1875 - 1937

© 1932 Editions Durand, Paris.
Reproduced by permission of Editions ARIMA Corp and
Editions Durand S.A./United Music Publishers Ltd.

The Pines of Rome
I pini della Via Appia

Text p. 37

Ottorino Respighi
1879 - 1936

William Tell

Text p. 38

Gioacchino Rossini
1792 - 1868

Symphonie Fantastique

Opening of 3rd Mvnt.
In the country

Text p. 38

Hector Berlioz
1803 - 1869

Symphonie Fantastique
End of 3rd Movement

Rob Roy Overture

Text p. 39

Hector Berlioz
1803 - 1869

La Damnation de Faust

Romance "D'amour l'ardente flamme ..."

Text p. 39

Hector Berlioz
1803 - 1869

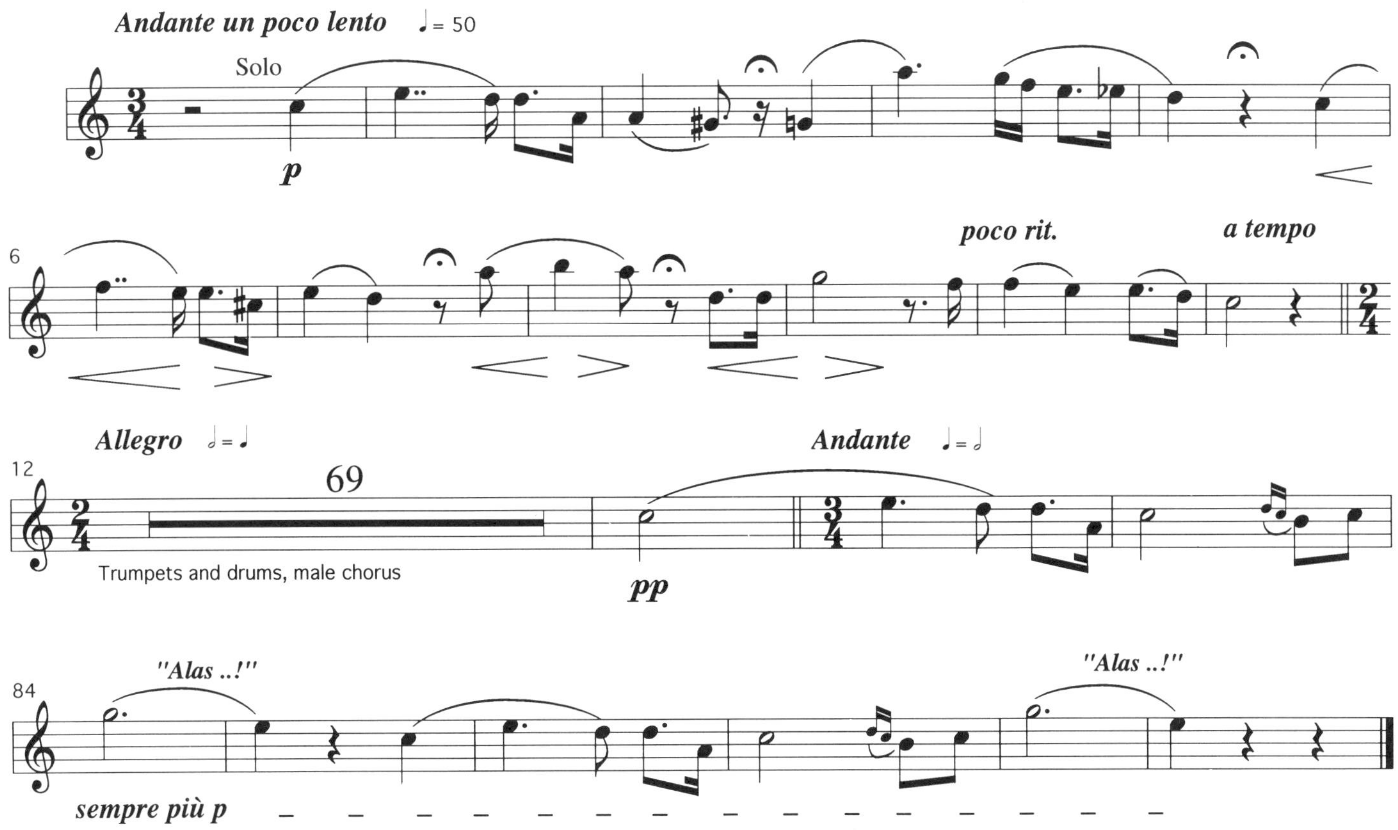

Symphony in D minor

Text p. 39

César Franck
1822 - 1890

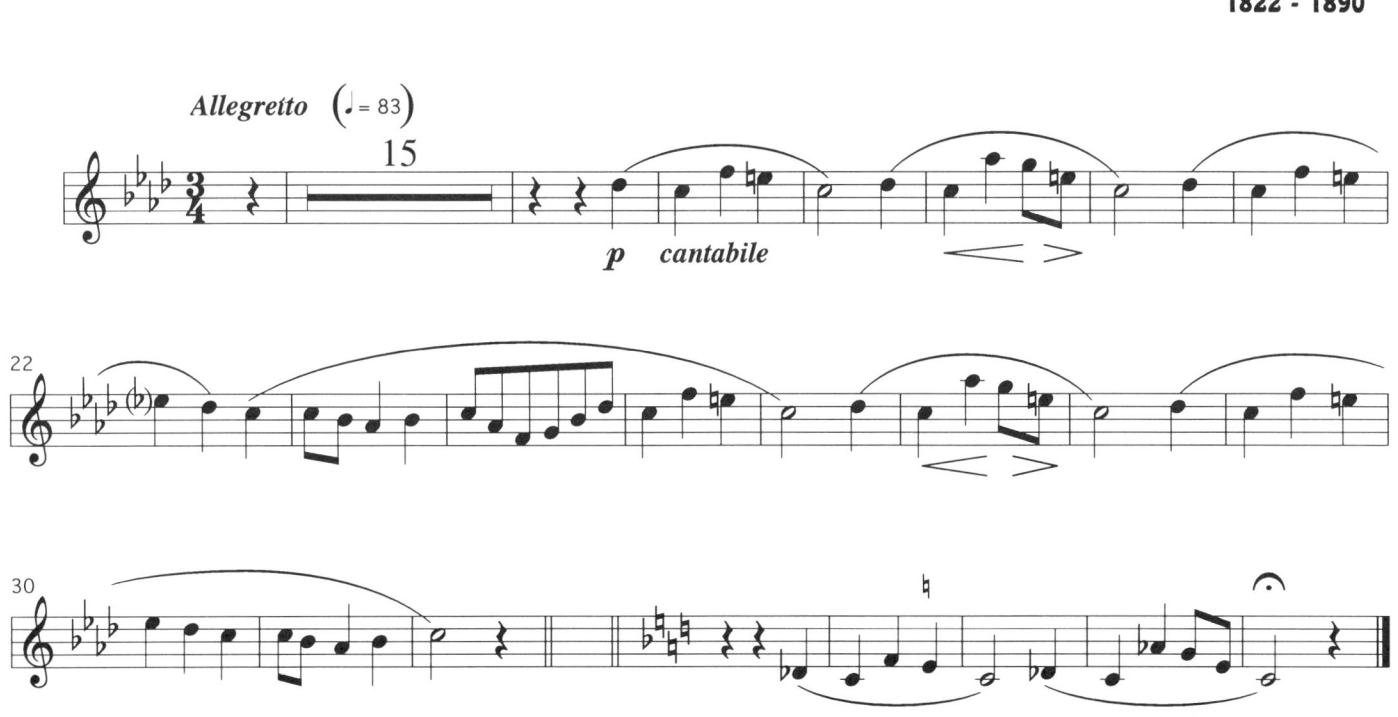

A Masked Ball
Solo from Act 2

Text p. 40

Guiseppe Verdi
1813 - 1901

Romeo and Juliet
Overture-Fantasy

Text p. 40

Peter Tchaikovsky
1840 - 1893

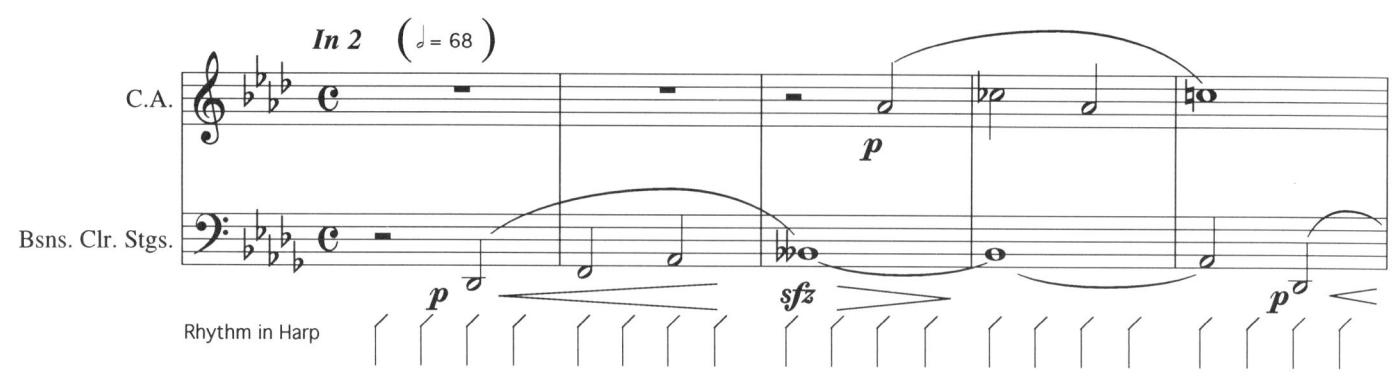
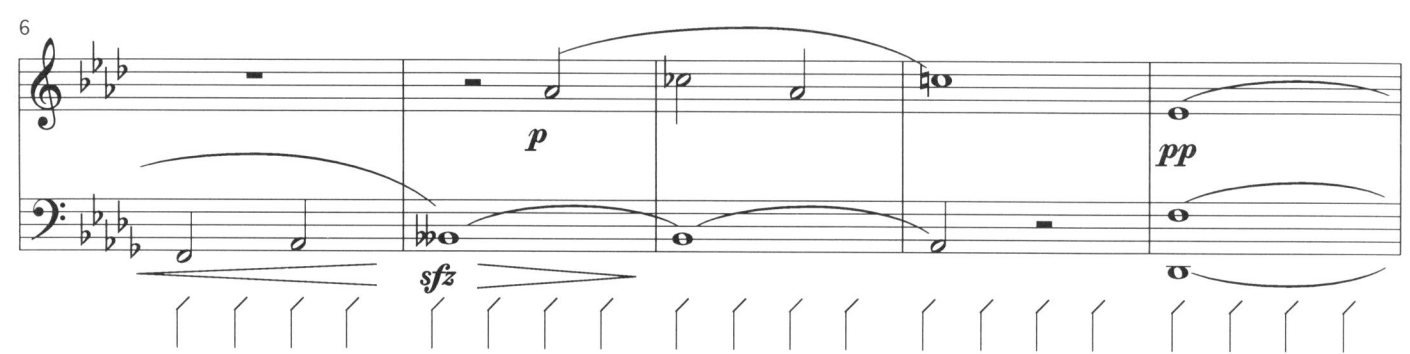
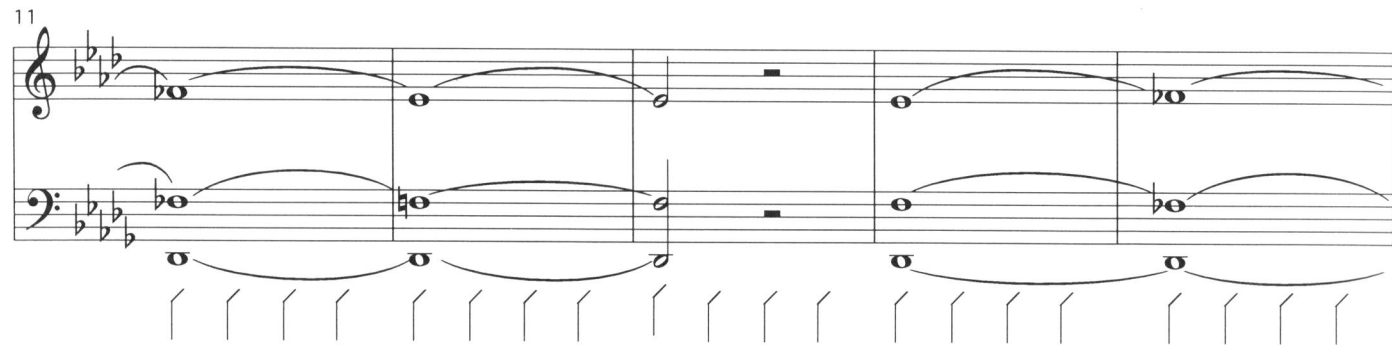
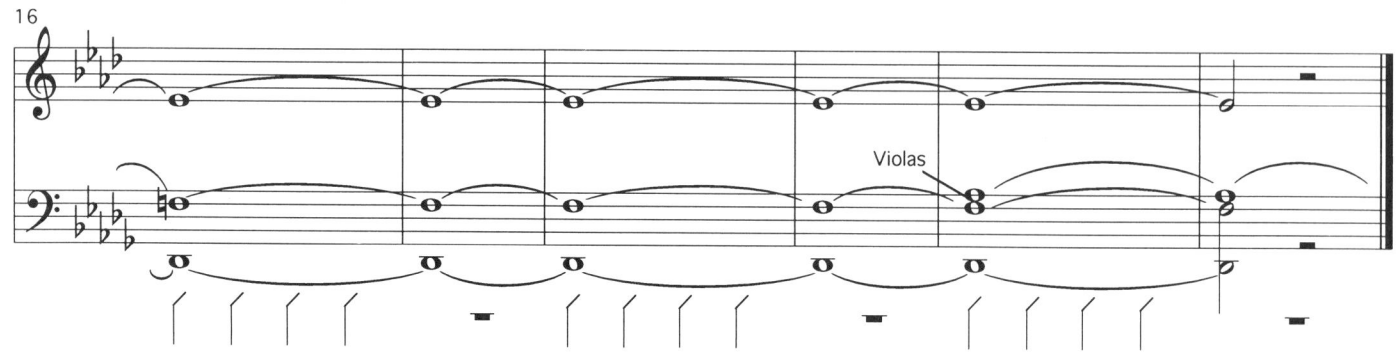

Symphony No 9 "From the New World"

Text p. 40

Antonin Dvorák
1841 - 1904

Three Nocturnes
1. Nuages

Text p. 41

Claude Achille Debussy
1862 - 1918

12
C.A.
Orch.
9
15
molto espressivo
p molto dim.
pp
19
Plus lent
bssns.

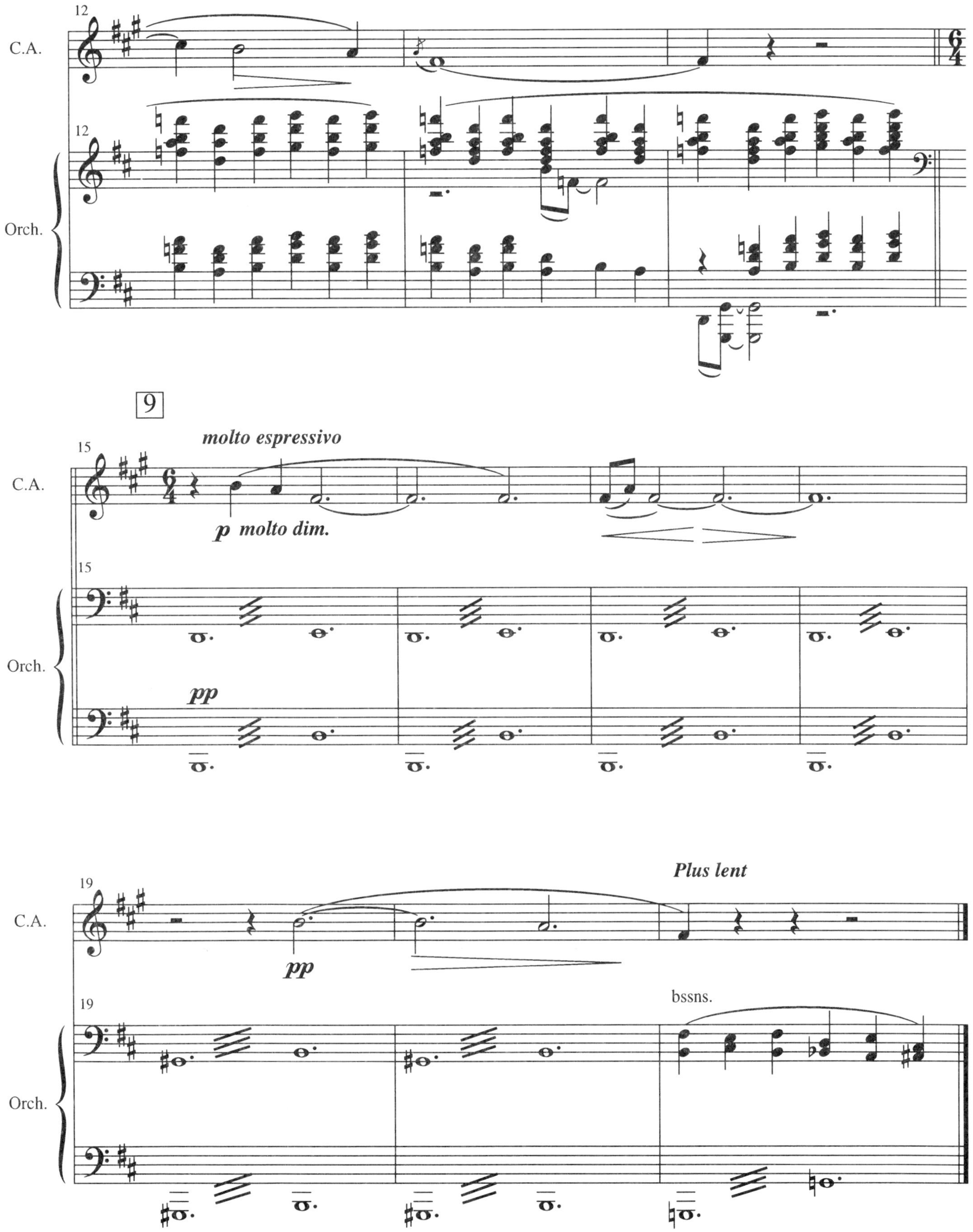

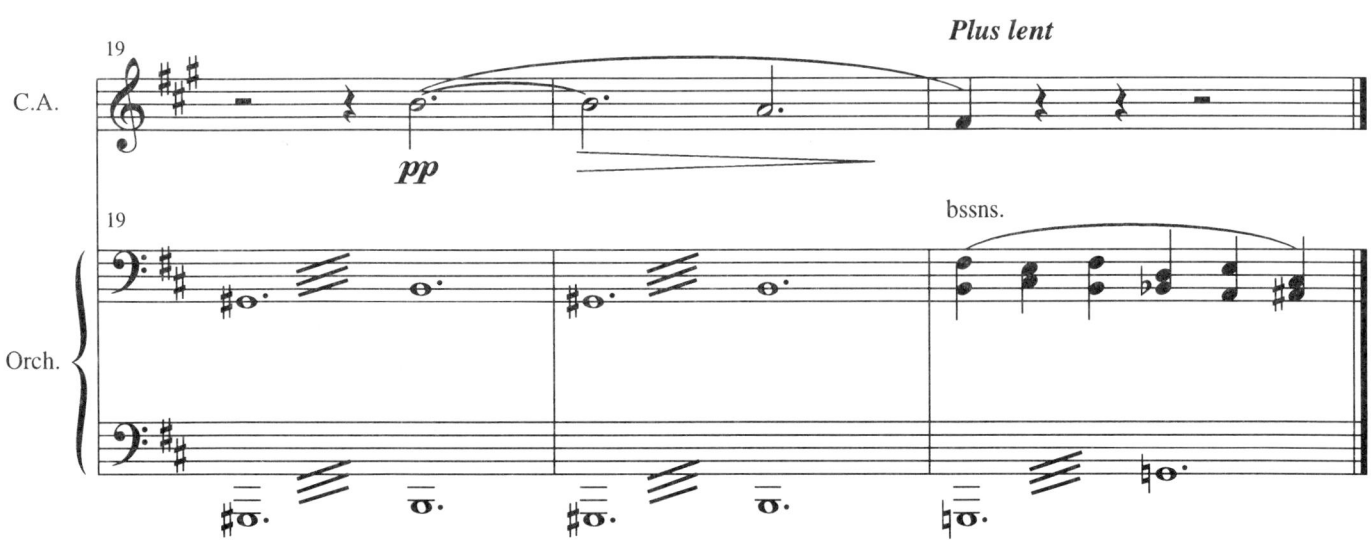

Three Nocturnes
2. Fêtes

Text p. 41

Claude Achille Debussy
1862 - 1918

Three Nocturnes
3. Sirènes

Text p. 41

Claude Achille Debussy
1862 - 1918

Modérément animé

Concierto De Aranjuez
for Guitar and Orchestra

Text p. 41

Joaquín Rodrigo
1901-1999

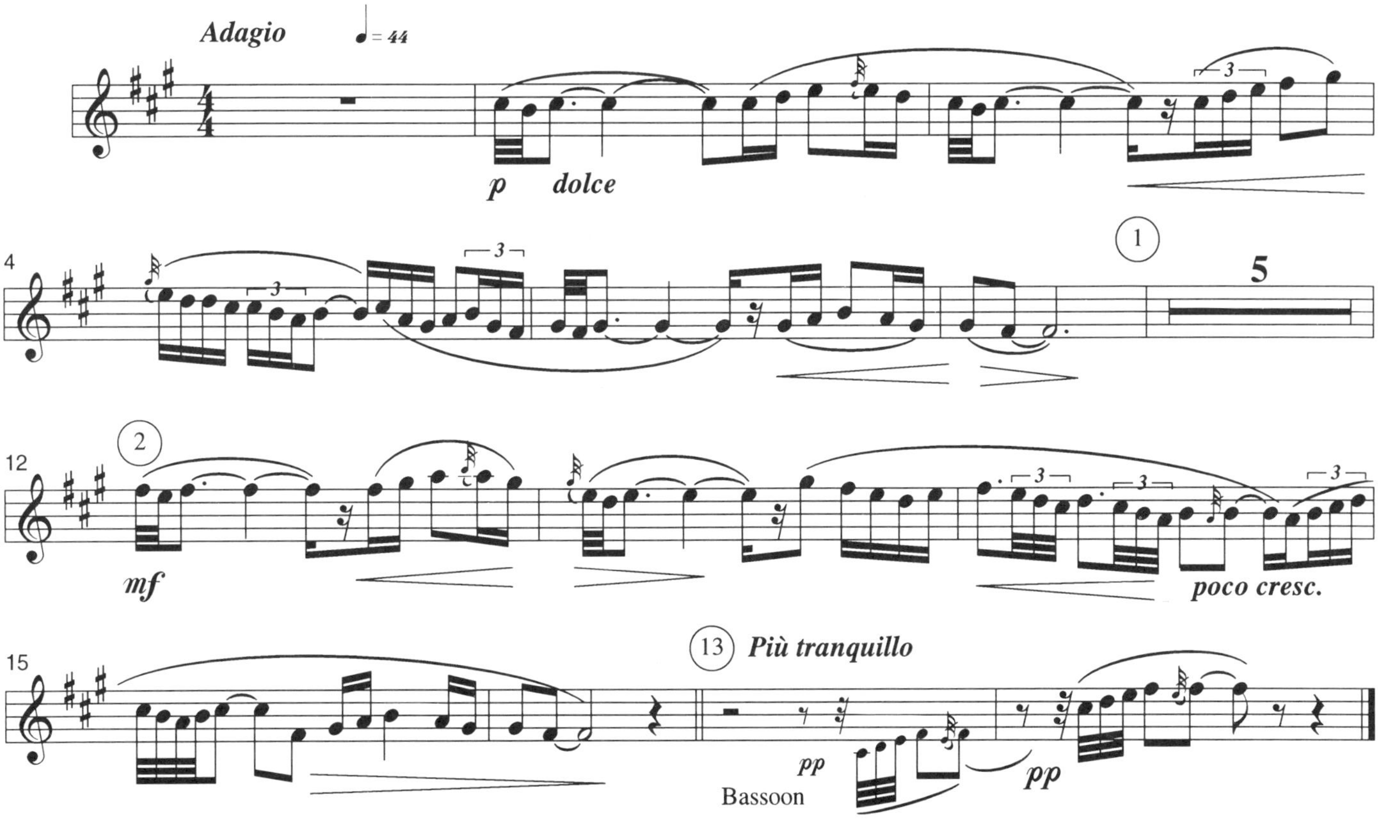

© 1959 by Joaquín Rodrigo, Madrid. Reproduced by permission of Schott & Co. Ltd (London)

Le Carnaval Romain

Text p. 41

Hector Berlioz
1803-1869

Muta in ob 2

La Mer

Text p. 42

Claude Achille Debussy
1862 - 1918

Rückert Lieder
"Ich bin der Welt ... "

Text p. 43

Gustav Mahler
1860 - 1911

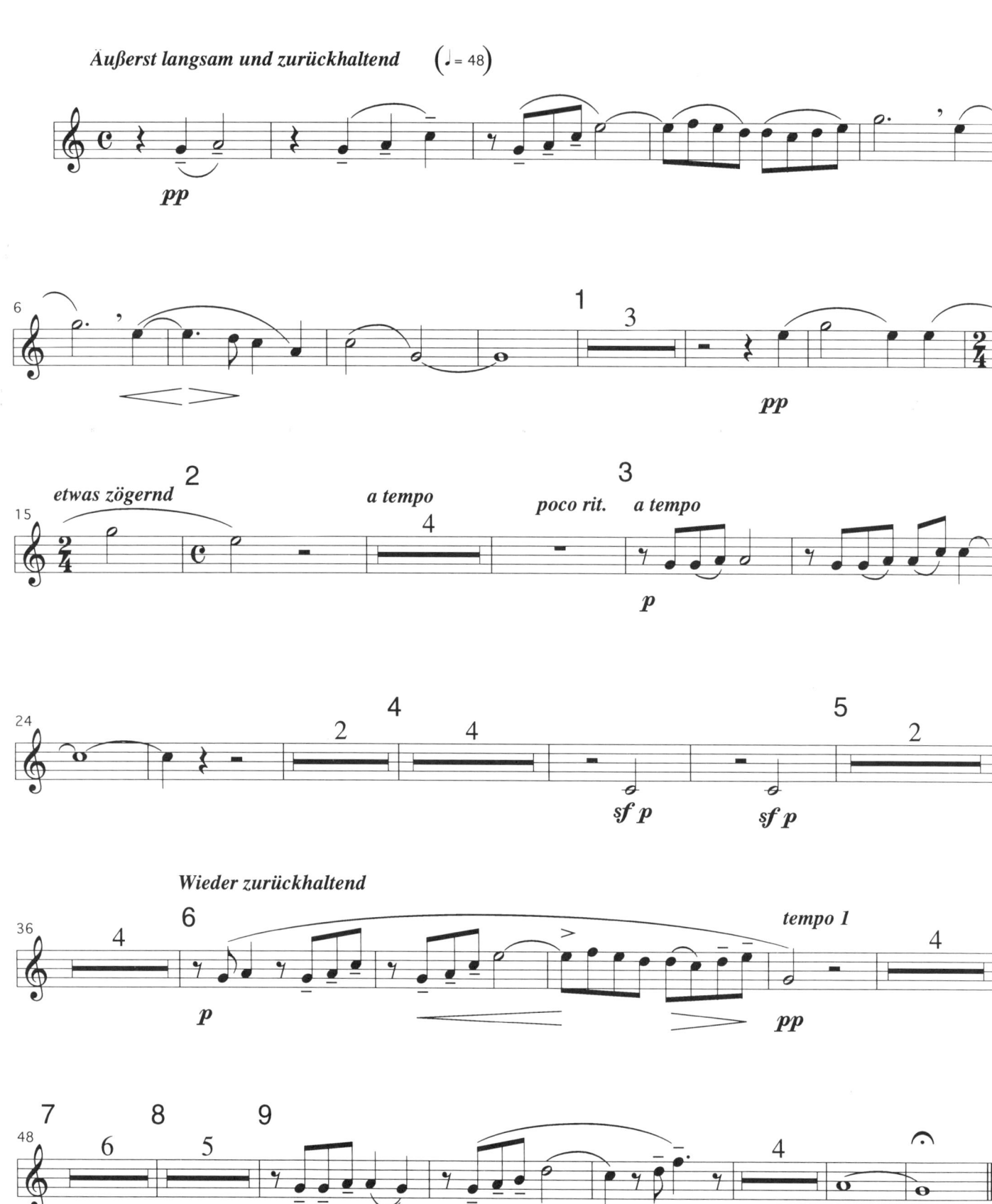

Kindertotenlieder
"Wenn Dein Müterlein..."

Text p. 43

Gustav Mahler
1860 - 1911

The Rite of Spring

Text p. 43

Igor Stravinsky
1882 - 1971

INTRODUCTION

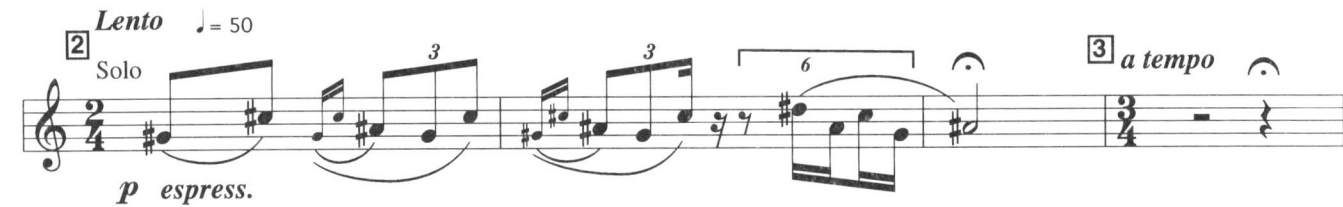

RITUAL ACTION OF THE ANCESTORS

© Copyright 1912, 1921 by Hawkes & Son (London) Ltd.
Reproduced by permission of Boosey & Hawkes Music Publishers Ltd.

The Nutcracker Ballet

Text p. 43

Peter Tchaikovsky
1840 - 1893

The Three Cornered Hat
The Miller's Dance

Text p. 44

Manuel de Falla
1876 - 1946

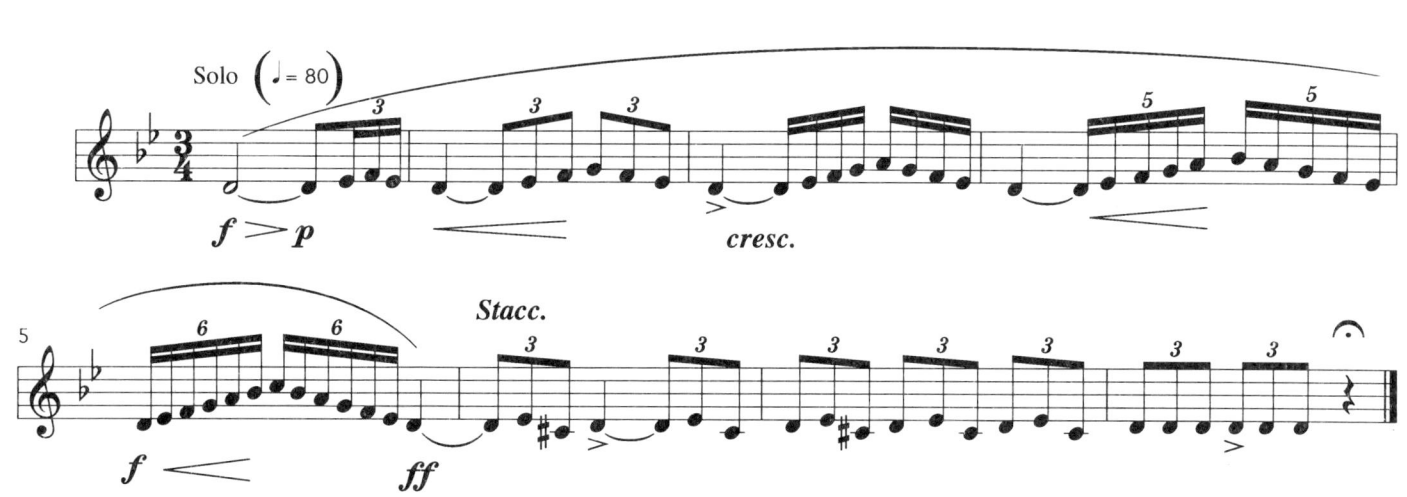

Reproduced by permission of Chester Music Ltd /
Manuel de Falla Ediciones

The Bells

Text p. 44

Sergei Rachmaninov
1873 - 1943

Nocturne
The Kind Ghosts

Text p. 44

Benjamin Britten
1913 - 1976

dying away

© Copyright 1959 by Hawkes & Son (London) Ltd.
Reprinted by permission of Boosey & Hawkes Music Publishers Ltd.

Reeds

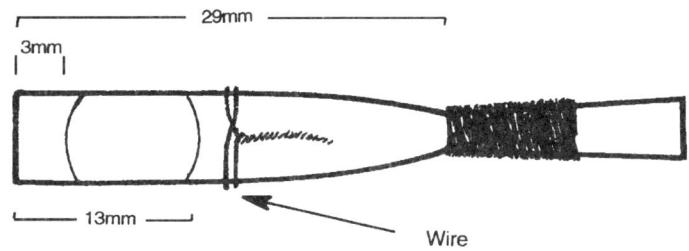

Many good books have been written about the making of oboe reeds, and I do not want to duplicate them here. What concerns me is how cor anglais reeds may differ from oboe reeds.

These ideas suit me, but of course there are many other designs that are just as good. I am not a great one for intricate measurements because I think reed making is more of an art than a science. In general, when people start making their own cor reeds they make them too big and have far too much wood in the reed, thinking this will give them a bigger sound. Such reeds are too hard to blow, are flat in the middle register and tend to crackle or make frying noises when they do a *diminuendo*.

I suggest a smaller reed than many people use and with a thicker tip than for an oboe reed, and more taken out of the back. If the shape is too big then the octaves will go flat. My concept of the reed is perhaps something nearer to a bassoon reed than to an oboe reed in the way it is scraped.

The gouge is .64mm and the width of my shaper is 8.4mm at the tip. The reed is tied on at 31mm from the tip to the top of the staple and then cut off to 28-29mm. If you use a narrower shaper then the length can be up to 30mm. It is no use measuring the overall length of reed and staple when you are dealing with cor reeds. It tells you nothing because some staples fit further onto the crook than others.

The scrape is 13mm and the tip is 3mm, but it is a good idea to avoid any noticeable bumps just behind the tip. You can take more out of the middle of a cor reed than with an oboe reed, but it must have a wire or it will collapse. The octaves will not go flat because of the little side vent on the cor which duplicates the G-sharp key. You do not have that on an oboe. The gouge bed is 12mm diameter and the blade 13mm diameter. Gouge the cane dry, using a little almond oil. A hand-held rounded scraper can thin gouged cane if you do not have a gouging machine. You can make a scraper out of a hacksaw blade, or just use a gouging machine blade on its own to thin the inside of the cane before you tie on.

With oboe reeds, people prefer not to use a wire if at all possible. I think it is true that a wire can interfere with the vibrations of an oboe reed, but for the cor reed, things are quite different and the wire can even be quite high up, almost at the halfway point. This also holds the reed together and seals it, if it has been shaped with enough care.

If your reeds crackle, as a desperate measure try cutting 1mm off the tip to make it thicker and then scraping back. Also, make sure there are no bumps in the scrape. That will improve things greatly, but we are still at the mercy of the cane itself.

Lastly, the bocal (crook) is of critical importance. If you are setting up a new cor anglais then try as many different bocals as you can. This could improve both sound, intonation, and the reliability of the instrument.

The Sling

Why not use a sling? The cor anglais is a very heavy instrument and it is a great strain to take all that weight on one thumb, especially if you are playing all day.

The cor will turn you into a lopsided person if you are not careful, and it will change the position of your right hand relative to the instrument. If you then try to play the oboe you may find you are pressing all the wrong keys, in particular the F key. Few people take notice of this advice, but if you develop bad habits it may be difficult to undo the damage.

When you are playing, use the sling to take only **part** of the weight of the instrument, and when you are resting you will also find the sling a great help.

The Swan of Tuonela p. 2   Jean Sibelius 1865-1957

Tapio was the god of the forest and Tapiola was his domain. But Finnish legend tells us of others who possess magical powers. Lemminkäinen is a hero and a mighty adventurer, a lady-killer and a warrior. He wishes to marry the daughter of Pojhola, and one of the three trials he must undergo is that he must kill the holy bird, The Swan, in the land of death known as Tuonela. But the Swan sings so beautifully that it is hard to kill. Lemminkäinen fails in the attempt and is cut to pieces by an old man who has been waiting for him by the river, but by magic his mother puts him together and looks after him.

The *Swan of Tuonela* was originally conceived as the overture to a larger scale work, an opera that Sibelius never completed. It was written in the last decade of the nineteenth century and it is possible that Sibelius, like many other composers, was strongly influenced by the cor anglais solo in Wagner's *Tristan* (q.v.).

One of the main problems in performance of this piece is that it is very static and lacking in rhythmical pulse so it is not always easy to know exactly where you are. Conductors should not underestimate the difficulties of achieving a good ensemble in this piece which relies very much on the conductor's sense of rhythm and good direction. Some conductors like to beat the first two beats of measures 5 as dotted half-notes and then sub-divide the last beat starting with the eighth-note triplet. I do not think this piece benefits by losing the shape of the phrases, and it is better to keep a feeling of three beats to a measure if you possibly can. Sibelius knew the cor anglais could not play an effective *fortissimo* high B and so in measure 18 it is doubled by the oboe. In measures 23 and 28 a sense of shape is most important in these rising figures. In measure 37 make sure the eighth-notes sound like duplets. Measure 49 is also doubled by the oboe and you might use the opportunity to take a breath before the descending scale in measure 51.

Glancing over the whole work just see how many slur marks Sibelius has put in. Particularly look at measures 40-43. To which phrase does the B natural in measure 41 belong? The previous phrase or the one following? According to the slurs it could be either. So if you were going to take a breath just there, would it be before the B or after it? A clue here is the Finnish language itself which does not favour up-beats. I would say the B belongs to both phrases and measures 40-43 should be played in one breath. But now cast your eye to measure 86. Here we have a similar problem: a B natural that seems to belong to both the phrase preceding it and to the one following. But where are the slurs? There are none. This one note hangs between one phrase and the next "as if fit for neither". It is isolated and could have a breath both before it and after. If you think that is crazy then just listen to the orchestral texture at that point. The gaps afforded by the two breaths allow the orchestral sounds to curl around this one note like mist rising from the river of death itself.

Tristan Act III p. 4   Richard Wagner 1813-1883

What would you say is the most difficult aspect of playing this piece? Think about it. Is it the breathing? Is it the fact that it is completely unaccompanied?

Let us assume you are going to do a cor anglais audition and have been told they are certainly going to ask you to play this piece. What are they looking for? I would say they just want to know if you can play the instrument, that you have a good command of the difficulties and that you are a musical player.

But there is more to this piece than that, for Wagner never intended it to be an audition piece. For him it is part of an opera, a piece of theatre. It is a shepherd's tune with a triplet feature (measure 31) not unlike that of the shepherd's tune in *William Tell* (q.v.). Both Rossini's version of the traditional shepherd's tune and the Berlioz *Fantastique* version were written in about 1829. The first performance of Wagner's *Tristan* was in Munich on 10th June 1865.

Perhaps there are two ways of looking at this solo, and that is what I was thinking when I asked you "what is the most difficult aspect of playing this piece?" My answer is "knowing whether to play it as a concert piece or as a piece of theatre in its true context". The two styles might be very different. How? Well, for a concert piece you are the entire show, with no supporting cast; in the theatre you are only one element of the drama, and off-stage for good measure.

For the sake of doing auditions let us first look at it as a concert piece:

After the opening statement (measures 3-6) it is perfectly feasible to take a good long breath. You can wait the equivalent of two whole beats. Before the *sfz.* in measure 10 there is another breath, and another before measure 12, this last one again the equivalent of two whole beats. In measure 17 take a breath before the C and another before the D-flat in the next measure, and again before the D natural in measure 18; before the A-flat in measure 19 and again before the A-flat in measure 20. The piece breathes quite naturally if you give yourself time. I would remove the slur from measure 23 to 24 and start afresh on the G natural (measure 24). Make a small gap after the second G in measure 24, not time for a breath. In measure 25, make the most of the falling thirds, giving plenty of sound on the F–sharp and F natural, and take another breath before measure 26 and another before 27. If you time these breaths right then they will sound quite natural and you won't be short of puff. Remember the low G at measure 29 is still *forte*. In measure 33, I would take a breath before the A-flat because the next few measures are arduous. If you can get to the D-flat in measure 38 then good for you, but remove the slur into measure 39, and take sufficient breath to recover before going on. Start afresh on the D-flat in measure 39. Take two breaths in 41, one before the A-flat and the other before the C. In measure 42 take breaths before the A-flat and before the F, and one last breath before the E–flat in measure 43. It helps greatly to play this piece from memory, because then you are less likely to panic over the breathing. It is a great piece, and may have set a standard in the mind of Sibelius and in the imaginations of many other composers as to the technical ability of the instrument and its dramatic association with the subjects of Love and Death.

Now let us look at it as a piece of drama:

The libretto says:- Act III. Prelude. *A castle garden. On one side a high building, on the other a long wall with a watch-tower. In the background, the castle gate. The castle is situated on a rocky height, with an extensive sea horizon visible. All is dilapidated and overgrown, suggesting years of neglect. It is day; hot and sunny. Tristan lies sleeping in the foreground, beneath a great lime tree. At his head sits Kurvenal, bending over him, grief-stricken. From without a shepherd's pipe is heard, an interminable desolate tune.*

So we have three elements in the drama, the idea of neglect, the grief-stricken Kurvenal, and the interminable, desolate tune of the cor anglais. It is quite important to separate the characters and make sure it is Kurvenal who is grief-stricken and not the shepherd. So now, the performance should perhaps be less sophisticated but certainly desolate and interminable. Perhaps it could have a sort of nagging coldness about it, more like somebody trying out reeds than being expressive and doleful as it might be for a concert performance. If anything the performance should contrast with Kurvenal's grief rather than be part of it, and the drama is in the juxtaposition of these two elements against the background of the dilapidated castle. The tune is transformed as Act III develops.

Ein Heldenleben p. 6   Richard Strauss 1864-1949

How old was Strauss when he wrote *Ein Heldenleben* (A Hero's Life)? One tends to think of *Ein Heldenleben* as a late work since, in this piece, he makes quotations from earlier compositions such as *Don Quixote, Zarathustra,* and *Till Eulenspiegel*. But these remarkable pieces were all written within the three years prior to 1898 and the composition of *Ein Heldenleben,* when Strauss was thirty-four. There also appears to be a quote from the oboe concerto, but the oboe concerto was not written until over forty years after *Ein Heldenleben*.

The extract I have given begins as the cor anglais emerges from orchestral texture and shows how the instrument has been playing continuously for eight and a half measures even before the solo begins, at measure 10. Not only that, but it continues without a break. More than one and a half minutes without a breath makes this a very taxing solo indeed. The quotation is from the composer's earlier work

Don Quixote and looks amazingly like the *William Tell Overture* (q.v.). Swiss shepherds traditionally play a similar yodelling triplet tune on the alpenhorn, to call in their flocks. It is hardly surprising to hear this shepherd's melody when one listens to his original cor anglais tune in *Don Quixote* because here the orchestral accompaniment deliberately sounds like the bleating of sheep. But why did Strauss write such long melodies for the cor anglais, and for the oboe in his oboe concerto? You have probably heard of a device called Samuel's Aerophon. A German flautist, Bernhard Samuel, invented a footpump that had an air tube going into the mouth for woodwind players. It kept them pumped up with air so they did not run out of puff while playing. Richard Strauss specifically asked for it to be used in his *Alpine Symphony* (1915). Did Strauss intend the aerophon to be used in *Ein Heldenleben*? No, because the aerophon was not invented till 1912. The oboe concerto was written in 1946 and by that time the aerophon would have lost its appeal, for it did nothing to solve the problem of a tired embouchure. It is more likely that Strauss got the idea of a long cor anglais solo from Wagner. Apart from anything else, Strauss was a technical genius. A master of his craft, I think it may be true to say that he expected everybody else also to be technical wizards. He had a predilection for long melodies. The theme at the opening of *Im Abendrot* (In the Sunset), from *The Four Last Songs*, may be the longest extended melody in the history of E-flat major, almost eternal. *Im Abendrot* was composed in May 1948, and though it is performed last in the sequence, it was the first of the *Vier letzte Lieder* to be written. The last was *September*, composed in September 1948. Strauss died in September the following year.

For *Ein Heldenleben* the best advice I can give to players who cannot use the technique of circular breathing is to ask another player to help out with the long notes. Some players use the B key to help the slur down to low D in measures 14, 15 and 19.

Eighth Symphony p. 7 — Dmitri Shostakovich 1906-1975

This solo from the first movement of the symphony, lasting more than three and a half minutes, must be amongst the longest of all symphonic woodwind solos. So if anyone tells you that a cor anglais player is a failed oboe player, then just let 'em have a shot at this tune.

This enormous cor anglais solo is heralded by one of the loudest, most exciting and thrilling of orchestral sounds. There is a deafening roll on the drums, fierce trills in the woodwinds, a fanfare on trumpets and trombones, and an almighty crash on the tam-tam. And then .... all goes very quiet ... and for a very long time. The strings continue their *tremolando* and this is the platform for this long and eloquent solo. The cor plays in quite a free, *recitative* style right up until the *poco più mosso* at measure 39. This is the main theme of the movement and from here onwards the strings play a pulsating syncopated rhythm that ties the solo player to more exact time values.

Just look at the metronome marks the composer has given us. It is probably all right to start at ♩=56 but in the slow triplets in measure 3 you might like to pick up the *tempo* just a little. In the 9/4 measure there is no *rallentando* marked, but many conductors ask for a big *ritenuto* and with a *diminuendo* going down to almost nothing. This can work to our advantage because measure 11 starts with a half-note rest and we can afford to take a breath in the slow *tempo* of the preceding measure. As always, a sense of story telling provides a structure for interpretation. Measures 12-14 seem to be asking the question "Why? Why are you telling me this awful thing?" ... and these measures can have a sense of urgency about them. Measures 15-17 are in a more relaxed *tempo*, more pensive as if to say, "I didn't expect to hear such bad news". Measures 18-22 say "I had such hopes of something more positive, but what you are telling me is really awful". In measure 22, pause as an actor would before he begins a new idea. Take a good breath and start fresh on the middle G. From measures 22-34 to music seems to say, "I must think of higher and better things, but really I want to scream, AND SCREAM, AND SCREAM" (these are the top E-flats, and the other woodwinds help you with these notes so you don't really need to play flat out). Measures 33 and 34 should sound really plaintive and lonely. Take a good long breath at measure 35 (before a new idea). Use a good singing tone from here onwards, for the return to the main theme has a feeling of warmth and resolution. I would not advise you to slur down to the low D in measure 39; even it you get it, a small *portamento* sounds really bad. Take a breath before measure 41, before measure 44, and before the D-flat in measure 46.

Experience is everything with this solo, and this is particularly difficult when performances of the 8th Symphony do not occur as often as one would like. It is one of the main problems of becoming a cor anglais player that you do not have opportunities to play the major works for your instrument as frequently as an oboist.

If you know you are going to have to play this solo then you will do yourself a great favour by learning it from memory. A miraculous 'chemical' change takes place in the brain when you know the piece by heart. It is like going into an exam, turning over the question sheet and knowing right away that you have passed. In other words it gives you a lot of confidence and it stops you panicking about where to breathe.

Tenth Symphony p. 8 — Dmitri Shostakovich 1906-1975

Do you remember the first time you tried this in the orchestra? You had a wonderful reed and the instrument had just been overhauled so it worked perfectly. The first two measures were fine, then you went for the low E-flat in measure 3 and nothing came out at all, very embarrassing. Why did it happen? That is always the question one asks oneself. I put it like this to you because there is a check I think you should do all the time during concerts and recordings. Is the F# / G# link properly aligned? If not, then you will not get your E-flat in this piece, nor in the *Rite of Spring*, nor in Tchaikovsky's *Romeo and Juliet*. Check that link again and again and again.

This extract from the third movement is the first time the cor anglais plays in the symphony; up until then you have been playing the third oboe part which, by and large, is fast and furious. This solo occurs quite late in the movement, which is rather quiet in style. There is no opportunity to warm up the instrument by playing. Your cue is a soft stroke on the tam-tam.

Piano Concerto in G major p. 9 — Maurice Ravel 1875-1937

Another lengthy melody for the cor anglais, this lovely tune presents special problems for the player. Firstly it is very slow, almost six in a measure, but definitely 3/4 rhythm. Secondly, the solo piano is playing a 6/8 rhythm in the left hand and a thirty-second-note running passage in the high register for the right hand. You need a lot of strength and stamina for this melody, especially when you go up to the high C-sharp. As to where to take a breath, the best thing to do is to follow Ravel's phrasing marks and put in breaths where you think a singer would if this were a song.

Very slow tunes need special care from the player of a melodic instrument. It is very important not to 'sit' on each quarter note, and to preserve a feeling of three in a measure, or even one in a measure, although the *tempo* is very slow. This gives the melody a shape and makes it sound 'airborne'. A similar tune appears in Honegger's *Concerto da Camera* for flute and cor anglais.

The Pines of Rome p. 10 — Ottorino Respighi 1879-1936

Respighi studied with Rimsky-Korsakov, wrote nine operas, many works for orchestra, transcriptions for orchestra, songs and choral works, but is probably best known for his two symphonic poems 'The Fountains of Rome' and 'The Pines of Rome', and for his masterly and exquisite orchestration. His combination of sounds is miraculous and there can be no doubt the composer intended to create pictures in the mind of the listener. In the last part of *I Pini di Roma*, 'The Pines of Rome', he asks us to imagine the Appian Way, the long straight road that leads into Rome. The *tempo di marcia* suggests to my mind a ghostly image of Roman legions returning from an arduous campaign. The tune for the cor anglais is curiously out of time with the march and suggests to me a chariot bumping over the stones and having some difficulty keeping up with the others.

The many *appoggiature* in the solo should be played in a lachrymose style, which is very Italian, and which also suggests perhaps the agonising weariness of a very long journey, and walking wounded.

For the player the main problem with this solo is the two descending passages in sixteenth notes with quintuplets right at the beginning. They are very chromatic and sound similar at first hearing, but in fact the note patterns are quite different. I advise players to learn these two phrases by heart so as to be absolutely sure of them, and that is why I have included this extract in this collection.

William Tell p. 11 — Gioacchino Rossini 1792-1868

Experienced players will notice that my version of *William Tell* is not quite the same as the usual printed orchestral part. In the original manuscript many of the slurs are missing and the last note of measure 33 is an F-sharp. We usually have an E in the cor anglais part. Rossini wrote an F-sharp (actually he wrote concert B), but most of the early printed scores have an E. So you can take your pick. Now look at measures 23, 24, and 29. These are Rossini's phrase-marks though they do not seem to appear in modern editions. If you take into account that this is the only tune the cor anglais plays in the entire opera then it is reasonable to suppose the composer wanted a special effect. I think the phrasings and the F-sharp are rather quaint. The tune itself is in the style of a traditional alpenhorn melody used by the Swiss to call in their flocks. The *Ranz des vaches* ('Ranz' pronounced 'Runts') is an idea also used by Wagner in *Tristan (q.v.)* and by Strauss in *Don Quixote* and *Ein Heldenleben* (q.v.) and by Berlioz in the third movement of his *Symphonie Fantastique* (q.v.), but here the melody is quite freely adapted.

If one were to play exactly what the composer wrote then many of the notes would be separated and I do not think that is right. In my version of the cor anglais part I have simply gone for a unity of style and have tried to stick to the composer's idea of something really rather special. My ideas are speculation of course, but so are everybody else's. I believe it is the responsibility of the performer to be equal to the composition, not its inferior. I believe my version to be very similar to the original orchestral parts. The earliest printed full score shows a metronome marking of ♪=76. This is a very good *tempo* if you do not like the flute player, for he has many more notes to play than you, but I have given a *tempo* of ♪=60 as being more representative of the way we are asked to play it these days.

Symphonie Fantastique p. 12 — Hector Berlioz 1803-1869

Perhaps it is somewhat extreme of Berlioz to expect the whole orchestra to be behind a curtain for the entire performance of the *Symphonie Fantastique* as he originally intended, but he does allow that the piece may be given at concerts too. His explanatory notes at the front of the score leave one more puzzled than ever, but fortunately we are allowed to dispose of them in the event that the symphony is not played as a melodrama, but as a concert piece.

Berlioz tells us that the third movement opens with two shepherd-lads playing the *Ranz des vaches,* a tune used by the Swiss shepherds to call their flocks together. His version of the traditional shepherd's tune is more freely adapted than in the versions by Rossini, his contemporary, or later by Richard Strauss in *Don Quixote*. The scene is pastoral and idyllic, but apparently ruined by the appearance of the composer's girlfriend whom he does not seem to trust, but who still manages to take up most of the music in the third movement. The movement ends with a sunset and we hear the shepherd-lad playing once more, but this time his friend does not answer. There is only distant thunder.

I have printed out the end of the third movement in full so you can see the timpani parts. Up until this time in history the timps were usually played with hard sticks in the military style. Here Berlioz asks for softheaded sticks and writes for timpani in no less than four-part harmony. For the cor anglais, measure 11 of the first excerpt, and measure 13 of the second have identical notes, but different phrasing and different dynamics; the shepherd-lad has realised his friend has gone. In measures 18 and 19 of the second extract he reassures himself that all is well. In the next measure, marked *perdendo* or 'getting lost', he feels a chill at the realisation of his loneliness. Only two notes left to play, and he feels that without his friend he is almost as nothing at all.

The cor anglais, like the harp, had been used before in musical ensembles by both Gluck and by Mozart, but in the *Fantastique* these two instruments appeared together for the very first time in a symphonic work. The *Symphonie Fantastique* was written in about 1829, and the cor anglais of that time would have been a simple structure with very few keys. This is not to say the contemporary instrument could not play faster melodies, for Berlioz went on to write far more elaborate parts for the cor anglais in *Harold in Italy*, the overture *Rob Roy* which is quite hard to play even on a modern instrument, the overture *Roman Carnival*, and *La Damnation de Faust* which contains one of the finest cor anglais solos in the operatic repertoire.

Rob Roy Overture p.14 — Hector Berlioz 1803-1869

Berlioz was unsatisfied with *Rob Roy* at first, and put the music aside. The overture only came back into the repertoire about thirty years ago, and even now it is less familiar than his other works. This solo is very exposed and shows that Berlioz must have been used to hearing the cor anglais played by a capable instrumentalist.

La Damnation de Faust p.15 — Hector Berlioz 1803-1869

If the *Fantastique* was a symphony designed for the theatre *La Damnation* was an opera designed for the concert hall, though the composer quickly tried to get it onto the stage at the Theatre Royal, Drury Lane. Perhaps it is true of all creative artists, and certainly true of Berlioz, that they seem to make a careful study of human emotions. Nowhere is that more clear than in the opening scene of Part Four. Marguerite is alone and waits for Faust without whom, for her, life has no meaning. She sings "the burning flame of love consumes my youth away". This is a long aria that begins with the cor anglais solo I have quoted. The cor anglais is featured throughout the aria which is interspersed and contrasted with drums and trumpets, and a chorus of revelling male students. The composer uses the same halting style at the beginning of this passionate monologue as he does at the opening of the first movement of *Symphonie Fantastique* (*Visions and Passions*), and also at the beginning of the third movement (*In the Country*). It is almost as though the character draws her or his ideas out of nothing and in pieces before trying to assemble them. This fragmented melody appears many times in the aria and is drawn together with many different harmonies and accompaniments as Marguerite tries to draw her life and her emotions together.

There is a perfect emotional progression in the construction of this melody. First measure, F major "Here I am and I don't feel too bad". Immediate reaction to that statement "I feel very stressed indeed" (the melody ascends by nine degrees ... and then descends). "Perhaps things are not so bad" and then immediately "I feel anguish". Next phrase "It'll all work out well / I know it will". At the end of the piece, the melody never reaches such heights of self-reassurance and Marguerite sings "Alas". The cor anglais has the last sentiment and plays a reduced version of the opening melody, but with a little twiddle in the tune. Isn't that how all such lonely monologues end? "I haven't sorted any of it out, so I might just as well sit down and twiddle my thumbs".

Once we have worked out a scenario for the piece, it can be worthwhile finding ways to project the emotions therein. *Vibrato*, rhythm, *rubato*, dynamics, pitch, quality of sound: these are the tools we can use to make the audience understand the train of emotions that Marguerite feels. Like an actor, we have to do more than just read out the lines. We must give a performance that is worthy of the composer. We must interpret it, and we must be equal to it.

Symphony in D minor p. 15 — César Franck 1822-1890

This is a highly individual tune. What is difficult about it? Cast your professional eye over it. The whole symphony constantly returns to the same melodies, and this tune constantly returns to the same note, our middle C, which is not the warmest sound on the instrument and which is difficult to match up with the other notes. Make a reed that plays the best C possible (and that means scraping out of the middle, and a reed that is thin at the sides) and put a stress on just about any note that is not a C. The phrase marks in the extract are as written in the score, but the C at the end of measure 22 is not meant to be tied to the C that follows it. This solo starts with an up-beat (pick-up).

Be careful to make sure you use a *vibrato* on the D-flats. It often feels nice to play an up-beat without *vibrato* and then play the next note **with** *vibrato*. It sounds terrible to the listener! As a general rule try to play **all** up-beats **with** *vibrato*.

The Willow Song from Otello p. 16   Giuseppe Verdi 1813-1901

Act 4 of *Otello* begins with an unaccompanied cor anglais solo setting the mood for an anguished monologue, which last almost twenty minutes. *Otello's* wife, Desdemona, recalls a song she heard as a child that tells of a woman whose lover has gone mad and who has deserted her. But it is not fate that threatens Desdemona so much as the evil machinations of the vengeful Iago. Technical perfection is the least of the requirements for the demanding cor anglais solo, which covers almost the entire range of the instrument. Only a small part of it is quoted in the music section of this book. Measure 40 is marked *ppp*. Some conductors ask for it *pppppp*, the quietest solo in history, and it has to be in tune. In the opera house, it is not at all uncommon for the cor anglais player to have to play massive solos towards the end of an opera. *The Willow Song* is one example, *Tristan* is another. In *Otello*, Verdi makes the cor anglais player wait for nearly two hours before the lights go down, the curtain rises, the audience falls silent, and the cor anglais plays ... alone. These circumstances can be a severe test of one's nerves.

A Masked Ball - solo from Act 2 p.17 Giuseppe Verdi 1813-1901

The setting is a lonely field on the outskirts of Boston. It was to have been Sweden but Verdi had difficulties with his producers, and so Boston it became. Act 2 begins with an aria for Amelia who is lonely and terrified, and so there is a solo for the cor anglais player, who is also lonely and terrified ...especially of the high E near the end. The solo begins unaccompanied. The second note of the solo, A_flat, is weak and needs a little help. The phrase at figure 12 that contains the high E, is doubled by the oboe 'for safety', but sometimes conductors ask the cor anglais to play alone.

Romeo and Juliet p. 18   Peter Tchaikovsky 1840-1893

The example I have given looks a little strange, but I want to point out that you need to listen to the rhythm in the harp. The *sfz.* in measures 3 and 7 generally throw the rhythm out, and make it difficult to know where to play the A-flat. Although it is often performed, *Romeo and Juliet Overture* is much harder than many conductors realise. In my experience the best orchestras play very close to the beat because it is easier and also because it gives the conductor much better control. Another problem with this piece is near the beginning, in the chords with the woodwind (not quoted). Here the cor anglais plays low Cs and low Bs while the flutes and clarinets are pitched very high. Clarinets are seldom at their best in the high register, especially clarinets in A. Perhaps the composer wanted a stressful effect. The opening of *Romeo* is quite hard for all the woodwind, and the funeral march at the end of the *Overture* requires perfect ensemble.

"From the New World" p. 19   Antonin Dvorák 1841-1904

I wonder how many conductors have noticed the marking in the score of ♩=52. I say this because there is a trend towards playing this, the *Largo* from Dvorák's ninth symphony, slower and slower. I think the fastest I have ever been asked to play it is ♩=40, and the slowest to date is ♩=26 and with many of the long sustained notes held way beyond their written value.

For that matter, I wonder how many cor anglais players have noticed the different dynamic marking when four measures of the tune return after the initial statement. Look at the position of the *forte* in measures 17-18 and 38-39 of the example. The first time the melody is played, the *forte* is on the B-flat, and the second time it is on the high C. It could be a slip of the pen of course, but I believe composers often want variety in the way we play their music and do not necessarily want a tune to sound the same every time it is played. Furthermore, if Dvorák had really wanted the tune to be played very slowly he could have written it at half speed as he does for the clarinet in measure 20. Measure 19 is played at the cor anglais *tempo* and in the next measure we have exactly the same melody, but at half speed.

If one considers this tune is based on a folk melody then it can be quite attractive not to play the dotted notes in too precise a rhythm. There are many ways of playing this famous melody, it is almost the 'Hamlet's Soliloquy' of the symphonic repertoire. You will need a lot of strength to play a good loud top C so make sure the reed is not too tough. If the shape of the reed is too wide then you may have difficulty with the intonation in the A-flat area.

Three Nocturnes p.20   Claude Debussy 1862-1918

Nuages beautifully depicts clouds in a moonlit sky by contrasting light with dark, and slowly shifting chords with contrary rhythms. At the beginning of the quoted example, the cor anglais plays four notes against six in the strings. Conductors usually beat six, so the player must be able to sort out the rhythms without help. *Un peu en dehors* means standing out from the background slightly. *Molto espressivo* at the end of the piece, suggests a dark and intense sound, not a wobbly *vibrato*, but you would not do that anyway, would you?

Fêtes are, in this case, nocturnal celebrations. But for the cor anglais player, it might be as well to stay home and practise some very fast *staccato*.

Sirènes are represented by the ravishing voices of the ladies' chorus. Ravishing cor anglais solos also are required. Perhaps the first three measures require a different form of *espressivo* from *Nuages*, something more romantic and enticing. The last two measures of the example are really sensuous.

Concierto De Aranjuez for Guitar p.23 Joaquín Rodrigo 1901-1999

The second movement of this wonderful *concerto* features one of the most famous and romantic melodies. The guitar plays spread chords to accompany the solo cor anglais. Style is most important here. It should sound romantic, austere, rhythmic, and Spanish. It is quite difficult to get a good balance between the first note and the second because C-sharp is a long-tube note, and B is short tube. In other words, the B tends to sound louder than the C-sharp, which is not what you want.

Roman Carnival p. 24   Hector Berlioz 1803-1869

I have always thought this to be one of the oddest of tunes, but played in its context it is really lovely. Listen to the viola eighth notes in measure 28 or you may be left behind on measure 29. Nowadays the violas wait for you. Phrase as printed in measure 34, and make sure of a powerful top B in measure 35. This is one of the weakest notes on the instrument so make sure it is you who plays the instrument and not the instrument that plays you. Some players give in to the naturally weak high register and never really try to overcome the problem. But what happens if the conductor asks you for a powerful high B? It is a good idea to have the technique to accomplish it even if you do not always choose to use it.

It is customary to change to oboe after measure 71.

La Mer p. 25 — Claude Debussy 1862-1918

It is quite hard to find a passage in *La Mer* that is **not** difficult and I would recommend anyone trying it for the first time to look at the whole orchestral score. Apart from the slow passage at measure 15, the symphonic sketches also contain some of the fastest passages for the cor anglais I have ever seen. But fast things can be practised at home. What is not so easy is to get the feel of how it all fits together in the orchestra.

At measure 15, there is in the score a metronome mark of ♩=104, but the *tempo* here is very flexible and the measures are often drawn out much longer, so it might be a good idea to practise it slower. Nowadays this passage is often played at roughly ♩=74. Two main difficulties: the first is that you have to play in unison with two cellos, which are a long way away so you cannot hear them. Secondly the melody is about two measures too long for comfort with the breathing, also it tends to become slower and slower and quieter and quieter (as it gets lower and lower). To keep perfect control over the last two measures is really difficult. It might be an idea to break the fourth to last measure (measure 21) for a breath; after all, the cellos continue the melody so the gap won't notice too much and also the two flutes come in there, giving a bit of cover.

The more you play *La Mer,* the more you will notice about it. In this piece, I think there is some of the most imaginative use of the cor anglais I have ever experienced. There has been nothing quite like it before or since. Debussy thought himself a realist rather than an impressionist, but in this matter he was alone in his views.

The example below is taken from the second movement *Jeux de vagues, (Animé).* There are also horns holding a pedal E, and *tremolando* strings, but this woodwind passage is quite prominent. The melody is in the flutes, and the accompaniment is in the clarinet section, the bassoon section, and the cor anglais 'section'. They rotate thus: clars./cor/bsns. - clars./cor/bsns. There is only one snag, there are two clarinets, two bassoons, ... but only one cor anglais ... so the cor has to play two notes to balance the others. The total chord at this point is E maj 7 with a sharp 5th. The grace note in the cor anglais part, which briefly reinforces the scarcely discernible E in the flutes' D# / E trill, is really quite important to the tonality of the chord. This is 'realism' by the deft touch of the master impressionist.

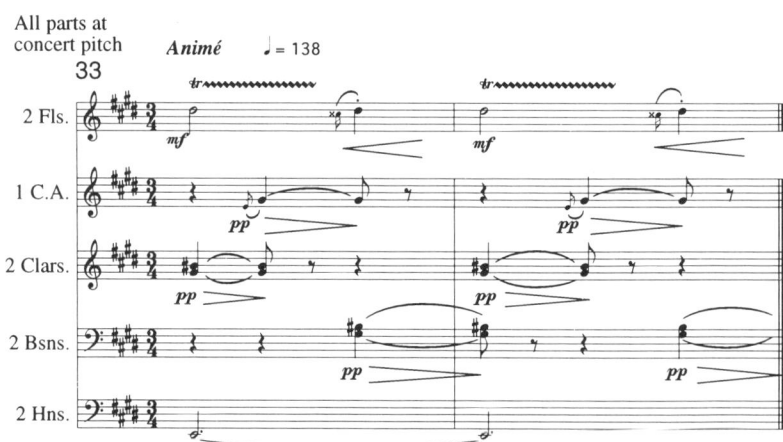

La Mer - Jeux de vagues

The point of this is to say, "do not play the grace note so fast that we cannot hear the pitch. It is very important". And also not so slow that it sounds overdone. Of course, in the score and in the orchestral material, the notes are transposed and the grace note is a written B going up to a D sharp.

Dialogue du vent et de la mer

In the above example, we have what looks like an *ostinato* accompaniment figure, but surely it is not, for this is a **dialogue**. It is a lead part doubled by one clarinet, it goes like the wind and with an enormous *crescendo*. Some say Debussy wrote *La Mer* while staying at Eastbourne, but the piano score was completed in Paris on 5th March 1905. He stayed in Eastbourne from July to August of that year.

Rückert Lieder p. 26   Gustav Mahler   1860-1911

"*Ich bin der Welt ..*" ("I have become a stranger to the world") is one of Mahler's most beautiful songs, and in the key I have quoted, it is a great gift to the cor anglais player. But, be warned, singers sometimes prefer it in a lower key. That makes it a lot more difficult for us. Also you may find this song in a cycle called *Sieben Lieder*, and you may have to play *oboe d'amore* in *Um Mitternacht*.

Kindertotenlieder p.27   Gustav Mahler   1860-1911

"*Wenn Dein Mütterlein ..*" is the third of a set of five songs on the death of children, a painful subject for Mahler whose little daughter had died of diphtheria. The markings *Schwer, dumpf* mean heavy and dull. This is a painful song, not at all romantic. The song is very sparsely scored at the opening, and since the cor anglais does not play in the first two songs, it can be difficult to make a really good entry at the beginning of the third. Compare the different phrasings at measures 5 and 37.

The Rite of Spring p. 28   Igor Stravinsky   1882-1971

These two short extracts are generally thought of as being the passages most in need of preparation. The first extract is difficult because of the grace notes, which go over the break on the instrument. The C-sharp grace note tends to sound muffled by comparison with the G-sharp. Does it matter when the notes are so quick? Yes it does. This passage can sound really garbled if the grace notes are played too quickly and are not matched in intensity. You need to be really alert to play this passage well, and that can be a problem when the *Rite* is usually placed in the second half of the concert programme. If you have had nothing to play in the first half of the concert then you may be quite sleepy by the time you have to play. Many people find the second extract harder because of the low Bs. If the instrument is working and your reed is all right then it should come out well. Be careful that the four notes leading up to the D-sharp are not like grace notes, they are in a very precise rhythm. Try to think in triplets as you come up to this solo. If the rhythms are precise then the passage can sound like a reptile slithering, as I think it should. If the notes are too quick, the phrase has insufficient definition.

The Nutcracker p. 29   Peter Tchaikovsky   1840-1893

There are more low Bs in *The Nutcracker Ballet* than in *The Rite of Spring*, so be warned. Some of the best tunes in the ballet do not also occur in the suite, and this one needs just a little attention. A wonderful piece to play, it is actually quite arduous, with a lot of high Bs which are never easy, and two slurs up to top D. Can your instrument do that? Are you sure?

The Three Cornered Hat p. 29   Manuel de Falla 1876-1946

One of the great things about the cor anglais is that you can have special reeds for certain effects. An oboe player often has to have one reed that plays everything. For this little *cadenza*, which is unaccompanied, I recommend the use of a reed that is larger than usual, has a much stronger wire on it and more wood scraped out of the middle. It is a good idea to use a larger reed because it does not matter if it will not play in tune in the octaves. The last six notes of this piece have caused mirth in the past because players' attempts to play an accent in *fortissimo* have produced a squeak and this tune has come to be known, rather unkindly, as "the taxi-horn solo". An accent in *fortissimo* is not possible; do not try. Did you know that in Flamenco there is no such thing as *accelerando*? .. only changes of *tempo*, and the *Miller's Dance* (after the cor anglais solo) is a Flamenco-style piece with four measures played at first slowly then repeated quicker and then at a faster *tempo* still. I recommend you use this idea in the *cadenza*. Play the first three measures with no *accelerando* then suddenly change to a faster *tempo* for measures 4 and 5. Put a pause on the second beat of measure 6 (which is a D). Take an enormous breath after the pause and really go for the *staccato* notes. No accent on the second beat of measure 8, but play the last three notes at twice the speed of the three preceding. That will give you the accent, but in Flamenco style. Spanish music is often very austere and strict in its rhythms. Particularly in Flamenco one should never stray far from that austerity, or it will not sound Spanish.

Experts have now agreed that there should be an A at the end of the second beat of the fourth measure, and this is how it appears in the extract. Thus we have a group of five notes instead of four, as in most orchestral material. The omission of this note in most orchestral parts is thought to have been an error on the part of the copyist.

Rapsodie Espagnole p.30   Maurice Ravel 1875-1937

Ravel was very fond of writing *cadenzas* for the cor anglais. There is a fine one in his ballet *Daphnis and Chloe*. In *Rapsodie Espagnole*, we have major solos that are almost *cadenzas*. The first is in the second of four movements (*Malagueña*); the other (in the fourth movement *Feria*) is perhaps not so much a *cadenza* as a solo in a very free style. *Rubato* can be very effective in these solos, though this has become less fashionable towards the end of the twentieth century when precision has become somewhat synonymous with style.

The Bells p.31   Sergei Rachmaninov 1873-1943

The Bells is quite a favourite with choral societies. The text is taken from a Russian translation of work by Edgar Allen Poe and the four movements depict respectively, spring bells, wedding bells, alarm bells, and funeral bells. It is no surprise to find a cor anglais solo in a symphonic work wherever the subject of Death arises. Rachmaninov's mournful tune is glorious to play, but you need to look at the notes.

Nocturne p.32   Benjamin Britten 1913-1976

Britten's *Nocturne* was written in 1958, and is a setting of poems on night, dreams and sleep. Each setting uses a different *obbligato* instrument: bassoon, harp, horn, timpani, cor anglais, flute and clarinet. The text for the cor anglais song is taken from a poem by Wilfred Owen, called *The Kind Ghosts* who prefer not to disturb their mistress. The string orchestra plays a very slow and ghostly march, while the cor anglais seems to drape cobwebs around the tapestries. This is a highly evocative piece that requires superb control on the high E right at the end. The third octave key on the cor anglais is really necessary here.

Circular Breathing

How to do it

Puff up your cheeks like a balloon. Now, holding this position, try to take a breath in through your nose without letting any air escape from the 'balloon' you have made with your cheeks. You probably find you can breathe in and out quite normally while holding your cheeks puffed up. If you can do this, then you have mastered the first stage of learning the art. This part is really quite easy. Practise breathing in and out while holding your cheeks puffed with air, and remember how this feels. This is very close to how it feels when you are circular breathing with the instrument.

Now take a reed, put it in your mouth and make it squeak just with the air in your puffed-up cheeks. The squeak will only be a short one because your cheeks can only hold a small amount of air. That is the second stage.

Put the reed onto the instrument and play a nice middle D in the ordinary way. Now things become a bit harder. Try to play the middle D using air in your puffed-out cheeks only, just as you did when you were squeaking the reed only. You can only make the note last about half a second, but that is just enough time to snatch a breath through your nose as you play. In other words, you are sustaining the note while you are taking a breath. If you can do this then you are doing pretty well.

The next stage is tricky. As the air in your cheeks runs out can you take over the blowing with your lungs in the normal way, so there is no interruption of the air stream? You probably won't achieve this on your first attempt, but now you have the general idea and with practice you will succeed.

The type of sound you make by blowing with cheeks is not as good as the tone you make by blowing in the conventional way with your lungs and diaphragm. You cannot really expect a seamless join between the two methods of blowing, but to become a master-craftsman at circular breathing the final stage is to ensure the pitch of the note does not alter as you change between blowing with your mouth and blowing with your lungs.

You will find that circular breathing is easier on some notes than on others. Some notes require more air than others do, so you should choose notes that require the least air. That is why I chose a middle D for learning. It would have been much harder on a low B. Try circular breathing on different notes to see which work the best. This will help you plan your breathing, as you should when you tackle a long solo. When your technique is perfect, then you may want to play every piece apparently in one breath, but I would recommend that you do not. Circular breathing can be rather a strain on the throat and anyway your embouchure needs a rest from time to time. But more than that, you yourself may appear not to need a breath but music often cries out for spaces which might as well be used for the player to breathe. There are only a very few pieces that require circular breathing, and so I would say that if you still find circular breathing a problem then forget about it altogether. Breathe in the conventional way, and put as many breaths into the music as you possibly can.

Historical Notes

The year 1720 seems to register the earliest appearance of the German *Wald hautbois*, which shortly became known as the *oboe da caccia* or *hautbois de la chasse*. The *oboe da caccia* had a flared metal bell and a large reed, almost the size of a bassoon reed. It was a curved instrument and had a pleasing, mellow sound, and played well in tune. When the flared metal bell evolved into the wooden egg-shape we now know, the instrument became known as the *corno inglese* and it appears in the scores of Gluck and Haydn, though Gluck replaced cors anglais with clarinets for his Paris performance of *Orfeo*. The concert trio by Haydn *Pietà di me* for two sopranos and tenor also features virtuoso parts for cor anglais, bassoon, and horn. Mozart wrote for oboes in F, called *serpentini*, in his opera *Ascanio in Alba* (K111), and for two cors anglais in the aria 'L'amerò' from the opera *Il Re Pastore*. There is also a huge *obbligato* in Rossini's *Messa di Gloria*. It was necessary to have very long fingers to play these ancient instruments because the holes were wide apart and there were few keys. The curvature of the instruments did however make the stretch much easier.

The music written for the cor anglais in the early part of the nineteenth century suggests the instrument at that time had good high notes and was quite capable of chromatic scales, though the *Rob Roy Overture* of Berlioz (q.v.) is quite hard even on a modern instrument. It has been suggested that there was a cor anglais in G, which would have made the high notes easier, but it seems this was pre-dated by the instrument in F.

The main transition to the instrument we know today was accomplished by the Paris firm of Triébert in conjunction with the oboist Barret, a Frenchman who spent most of his life in London, but who died in Paris, in 1879. The Barret-Triébert cor anglais was made of thin wood and was very light, in spite of having many silver keys. The sound also was light and sweet, and extremely beautiful.

Everybody wants to play the Donizetti *Concertino*, but the reason I do not recommend it for auditions is that it has so many high Es in it, and the piece does little to show off the middle and lower registers of the instrument which are by far the best. Many instruments do not play high E with any degree of comfort, and some not at all. The Hindemith *Sonate* is a major work for the instrument, but that has a very hard piano part and some difficult rhythms. One piece that lies well for the instrument and might do well at auditions is the Saint-Saëns *Swan,* which was originally written for the cello. I see no shame in using transcriptions if they show off what you **can** do rather than what you **cannot**.

For Composers

Orchestral cues for the cor anglais should be written at concert pitch and at the correct octave, but in F if you intend the cue actually to be played by the cor player in an emergency. Cor anglais players tend to think in concert pitch so cues for clarinets in B-flat or A are very confusing. If you write a cue for clarinet in B-flat and then transpose it up a fifth then the cor anglais player needs a computer to work it out. This is also true of violin parts that are transposed up a fifth and down the octave.

Try to avoid tunes that start on a very quiet low E (concert A below middle C) or low D. However, the middle and lower registers of the instrument are the best. The high register is weak and is often doubled as in the Sibelius *Swan of Tuonela* and Shostakovich *Symphony No. 8*. Not every player can use circular breathing technique so try to put in a few breaths for the player from time to time. Members of the audience often complain if they see a wind instrumentalist playing continuously without a breath because they tend to hold their breath in sympathy with the player and become exhausted. You might find that hard to believe but it is true.

The cor anglais can play many things besides shepherd's tunes. The cor part of *La Mer* covers the widest range of imaginative use of the instrument I can recall, and stretches the player's ability to the absolute limits within classical structure. And it is to be regretted that there is usually only one cor anglais in the symphony orchestra because the larger oboes sound wonderful in pairs or in 'choirs', a feature much appreciated by J.S.Bach, who wrote for *da caccia* in C and in the alto clef. This can be tricky to read, and even today it is occasionally encountered in some of Bach's *cantatas*.

Quite often the cor anglais does not play as part of the oboe section at all, and is used to reinforce trombones and bassoons, as in the third movement of Shostakovich's 8th symphony. Another good example of orchestral writing for the cor anglais can be heard in Wagner's *Parsifal*. Frequently the cor anglais blends with clarinets and bassoons, as in the very opening of the opera. The composer uses mostly the middle and lower registers of the instrument, which are the best. The player can often tell when the composer has a clear concept of the instrument in his mind.

I am aware that there is a lack of late-twentieth century music in this book. At the time of writing it is difficult to know which pieces are going to become standard repertoire. There may well be some orchestral solos that are significantly different from oboe solos, and should have a place in this book, but, as yet, they have not come to my attention. Although there are some fine modern *concerti* written for the cor anglais, the instrument seems to have faded as a notable orchestral voice, with the possible exception of film scores, where the association of the cor anglais with themes of Love and with Death seem evergreen.

Middle D, A-flat / Low E, E-flat, D/ Low B-flat

On many instruments, middle D is flatter than the D on the oboe, so the player must compensate. Low E, E-flat, and D often present more problems on the cor than on the oboe, especially when it needs to be very quiet. Scraping the heart of the reed helps the lower notes.

Pieces with quiet low Es you should watch out for are: - Mahler's 1st Symphony, and his *Das Lied von der Erde*; *The Four Last Songs* of Richard Strauss. Also, if I remember correctly, the *Queen Mab Scherzo* from *Roméo et Juliette* by Berlioz has 32 low Es. ... Enjoy. *Death and Transfiguration* by Richard Strauss has some very quite E-flats near the beginning. Conductors sometimes pull a face at that. Quiet low Ds are required for Mahler's *Kindertotenlieder* (q.v.). Middle A-flat tends to be weaker and less stable on the cor than on the oboe. A reed that is too wide and has a bump in the middle will not favour middle A-flat.

Both Mahler and Elgar wrote low B-flats for the cor anglais. For this, you need an extension between the lower joint and the bell. The most famous low B-flat for the cor was written by Mahler in *Das Lied von der Erde*. The composer instructs the player to play a B natural if the B-flat is not available. Some German instruments have a B-flat built on, as it is on the oboe. Such instruments are more than two inches longer, which makes them even heavier, and the extension alters the quality of some of the middle-register notes.

Water in the Octave key

The problem of water in the octave key beleaguers many cor anglais players, but in fact, the instrument should be no more of a problem in this respect than is the oboe. Firstly, make sure when you put the instrument away each day that the octave pipe is dry, otherwise the water will still be there the following day. If this fails, then (using the correct tool) take the octave insert out of the instrument and make sure there is no dirt present. Also, see that there is no scale on the metal. Scale appears as a brown stain. This should be removed with some kind of mild abrasive, and the metal should look bright. Then take a pipe cleaner, and with mild detergent clean the octave box and the tube around it. A detergent will help to stop droplets forming. Recorder players use this technique on the head joint. As a last resort, you should take the instrument to a professional repairer and ask him/her to flatten out the cup at the lower end of the insert (which you can only see when the insert has been removed) so that it is square and not cup-shaped. The cup has a tendency to channel the water into the pipe. In the drastic remedy I have just described, the length and diameter of the octave pipe should remain unchanged, and the sound of the instrument unaltered.

Intonation

Intonation is not just a matter of hearing, it is also a matter of knowing.

Anybody joining a symphony orchestra without realising that currently we use two types of intonation is going to have a hard life. The two types are of course Well-Tempered Intonation and Just Intonation. Well-Tempered (or Equal Temperament) is that which the piano and other tuned instruments have to use. The rest of us, who can adjust the pitch of our instruments as we play, use Just Intonation. You will soon see that the systems are not compatible and yet we use them both concurrently, therefore it is physically impossible for certain things to sound perfectly in tune. If you can accept this then you will retain your youth and good looks for very much longer than otherwise.

Would you like a demonstration of the two types? It is easily done, but you must have access to a keyboard instrument that you consider is well in tune, a good piano or a synthesiser.

Firstly, play a bass note, perhaps C an octave below middle C on the piano. Now you need to clear your mind of all distractions and think of the note one tenth higher than this bass C, that is the E above middle C. When you have got it clear in your mind then hum it so you can hear a perfect major third (plus an octave) with the bass C. While you are humming an E that is perfectly in tune with the bass C, play the E on the keyboard. You will notice that the keyboard E is quite a lot sharper than the E you are humming. All major thirds in Equal Temperament are sharp. The ear prefers a smaller interval and tunes the major thirds flatter until they sound 'sweet'. So how do we iron out this problem when we are playing? Practise with a tuning machine set to drone on a pedal note, then play your scale slowly from this base note and listen to each interval. Tuning perfectly by ear in this fashion gives you Just Intonation. If you simply tune each note to each note on the tuning machine you will have Well-Tempered Intonation and will have a tendency to sound sharp in the orchestra. If all else fails then there is that magic ingredient called *vibrato*. Use it with care and imagination.

If you are a science student and you want a really spectacular demonstration of how perfect intonation is physically impossible then there is an experiment I can give you that will leave you totally convinced. For this you need a harpsichord that has only one string to each note and which can be tuned with a tuning-handle. First tune the A to A=440. Now tune the E above it to what your ear tells you is a perfect fifth. When it is in tune, then take the E as your basic note and tune the B so it is also a perfect fifth higher than the E. When this is perfectly in tune take the B as your basic note and go down one octave so you have a B next to the original A. From this B tune the F-sharp, and from F–sharp to C-sharp. Go from the C-sharp to the G-sharp, and then go down an octave. If you continue in this fashion of tuning in fifths and octaves only then eventually you will have covered every note of the chromatic scale. Each interval will have been tuned perfectly. Now play a chord, any one will do, and I guaranteé you will hear the most out of tune racket imaginable. This illustrates a very important rule that if you proceed logically, after many steps, eventually you will arrive at an illogical solution. This is true not only in physics but also in some people's philosophy. To avoid this dilemma we use our intuition. The human spirit steps in and puts it all right.

Prior to J.S.Bach's pioneering of the Well-Tempered keyboard in which the out-of-tuneness was averaged out over the entire range of notes, church organs and harpsichords were tuned sweetly to home keys such as C major and D minor. This meant that remote keys such as F-sharp major were appallingly out of tune. Is it a coincidence that Bach chose that very key for the thunder and lightning chorus in the *St. Mathew Passion*? Probably he used a Well-Tempered keyboard, but there would still be an association of ideas with the bad old days when organs could only sound earth-shatteringly appalling in F-sharp major.

One can make a note slightly flat to make it sound dull or gutsy, or play it sharp to give it a bright edge. This is for solos, but in woodwind chording we have to use sweet intonation, and to a large extent try to ignore what the keyboards are doing. Also, we must be aware of the limitations of woodwind instruments. Some notes are very hard to adjust, such as low C sharp on both oboe and cor anglais. Other instruments have their problems too, but they will leave it to you to guess what they are, and you must try. Flutes go flat when played too quietly, and clarinets go flat when played too loud. It is worth bearing that in mind if someone accuses you of being sharp. Also, one should consider that the second harmonic (8va + 5th) in the cor anglais spectrum is more powerful than the fundamental. This is very confusing to the ear, and often confuses tuning machines as well.

In a woodwind section, the subject of intonation can be very thorny and has a tendency for people to find a scapegoat. Confidence is a great thing, but by challenging other people's intonation you are really challenging their judgement. If you do that, then you undermine the very mechanism that is required for good intonation, and, for that matter, for good ensemble. Good playing in the woodwind section is achieved by people who know, who listen, and who tune their *own* instruments.

To summarise then, one could say intonation is something that can only be optimised, it is seldom an equation that can be solved. It is an art, not a science. It is a matter of knowing as well as hearing.

Acoustics and Recording

How often have I sat in the recording studio and heard "Can we have more cor anglais? We can't hear it"? Many times. If you look at the seating in the recording studio you will often see the cor anglais player sitting close to the principal trumpet, so the microphone set up for the loudest instrument in the orchestra also has to do for one of the quietest.

Often, in addition to distance mikes, there are two microphones in front of the woodwind. This means the bassoon blows straight into the mike and the tone of the cor anglais, which bounces much of its sound off the floor, goes right past it. Thus pieces such as the duet for cor and bassoon in Tchaikovsky's *Capriccio Italien* may be hopelessly out of balance on the recording although it sounds all right in the studio. It depends how much they use the woodwind mikes and how much the distance mikes are used.

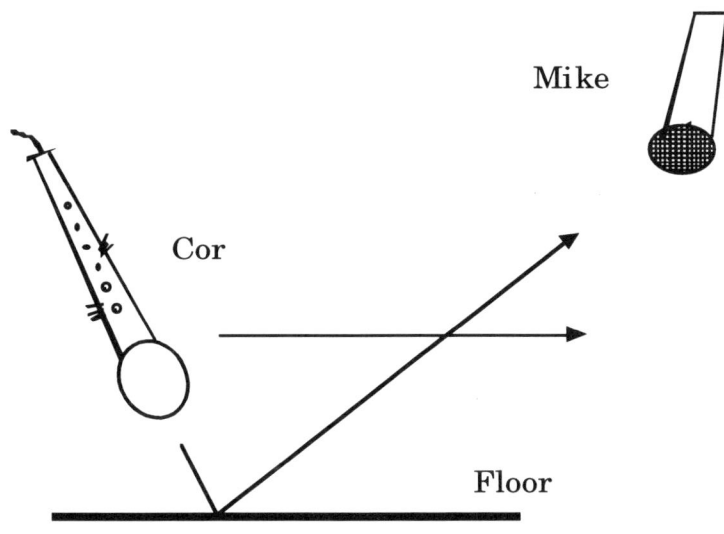

The diagram tries to show how part of the sound is bounced off the floor and part goes directly outwards. You notice there is a crossover point. Here one sound source can interfere with the other and actually cancel it out, so you have a note that won't record. It can be helpful to wear earphones so you can hear exactly what the microphone hears and adjust the position of the instrument accordingly so you do not have these 'blind' notes.

A directional mike pointing downwards to the floor so as to catch only the reflected sound can help eliminate keywork noise, so can the use of a dynamic microphone which does not respond well to loud noises of very short duration. Two microphones are much better than one, and sometimes you can adjust the position of your chair so you blow towards a mike, and not past it.

In the concert hall you do not just play the instrument; you play the building, moving the instrument slightly in one direction or another to catch the best resonant spots.

One of the hardest aspects of playing the cor anglais in the symphony orchestra is knowing how loud to play and it is a good idea to ask people how it sounds from where they are. Generally, if you guess how loud you think it should be and play just a fraction louder than that then you are probably about right. On solo long notes such as the long E-flat in the Tchaikovsky's *Romeo and Juliet* (q.v.) you should never play so quietly that you cannot do a *vibrato*.

The Performing Artist

At some time in most people's careers, whatever they do, they take stock of their chosen profession and think to themselves "what on earth am I really doing?" After all the philosophising, for professional players the answer is simple "I am trying to make a living". And then you might ask, "why am I a cor anglais player and not a principal oboist?" The answer to this lies mainly in chance, the opportunities available at the time and the quality of your instruments. To anyone who finds they are the cor anglais player in a symphony orchestra one thing is perfectly plain, that he or she is one of the principal soloists in the company. Likewise, it is also clear to everybody else.

When you are making your living, then the criteria for playing are that firstly it should be of a high standard, and secondly that it should be consistent. Anybody can make a mistake and this is forgivable, but in general, the standard must be consistently high. For this, you need technical ability and confidence. Sometimes life can be turbulent or concert conditions unfavourable, and these factors can undermine one's confidence.

It has been said, back in the nineteenth century, that "perhaps no person can be a poet, nor can even enjoy poetry without a certain unsoundness of mind, if anything which gives so much pleasure ought to be called unsoundness." And it needs to be said that if he is the sort of artist who needs to go down to the South of France and cut off his ear before he can create art then such a person will hardly be suitable for a symphony orchestra. A professional musician has to produce exactly what is wanted, precisely when it is required, and often to other people's standards. This can be very stressful. One can wander around "vales of golden daffodils" to the heart's content and dream up all manner of artistic ideas, but when it comes to the concert hall you are a technician, you know how to control your playing and you know what to do if something goes wrong. As of all professionals, more is expected than would be from somebody who just plays the instrument for fun. Try to find *different* ways of playing tunes, to keep them alive, unexpected, and interesting. Try to avoid formulae for playing music, for a formula in musical interpretation is as painting-by-numbers compared to art. Standardisation is a twentieth century concept, a product of the industrial revolution, and may not be appropriate for earlier pieces.

For the sake of argument one could say there are two types of artist, the creative and the performing artist, but immediately one will discover that all performers are to some extent creators and all creators are to a degree performers.

As a performer, you must concentrate on your breathing. Not just in taking breaths in the right places and in a way that suits the music, but you must learn how to breathe in the few seconds just before you have to play. You should make yourself breathe slowly and regularly, and not very deeply. You should try to breathe in the same way that you would when you are at home and relaxed.

There is a natural tendency to get very excited before a solo and also to be very apprehensive that it may not go well. The most common cause of anxiety is a bad reed or an instrument that won't work properly. So constant maintenance of instrument and reeds is obviously very important. Clean out your octave keys and check your F# / G# link. As for excitement, it is really quite important to keep your heart rate down, especially before very slow solos. You do not need drugs for this, just learn to control your breathing. Breathe not too quickly and not too deeply. You will find your heart rate remains steady and you will retain a good control of your solo.

No Air on the A String p. 52

Developing the concept of playing the cor anglais.

You may well think the piece on page 52 has the most boring melody ever written, to which I might say that you are probably right, but … it depends how you play it. Not only does this tune keep returning to the same note, it seldom leaves it. This exercise was devised for students who had never before made music in ensemble with another instrument and who had not considered the idea of changing the expressive quality of the sustained note in response to changing harmonies and musical registers around them. My original idea had no melody at all save one single note for certain of my students to play. Tethered to a concert A, they were utterly bewildered by the various sequences of chords I played on the piano. The example I have given is only an illustration, for you can probably think of other chord sequences that you may prefer. It does not really matter what chords you play, but some should be consonant and others dissonant, some high and others in the low register. The student can just hold a single note. The student should be asked if the note feels any different when it is accompanied by high sounds rather than by deep tones. If the answer is No, then probably that is the end of the matter, but if the idea catches the imagination then you could ask, "Do the changing harmonies conjure up any pictures, or sequences of pictures, in your mind?" Probably not straight away, but try simple ideas like "Are they warm or cold, tense or relaxed? Do you feel a sense of change in the harmonic progressions? If so, where and what sort of change?" Develop the discussion along these lines and then ask, "What can you do with the sound to become part of this little 'drama'? Can you make the sound warmer or more *'agitato'*? The elements you have at your disposal are Loud or Soft, Flat or Sharp, Fast or Slow *vibrato*, Quality of Sound, and combinations of all these". As you play a middle-E, think of the vowel-sound in the word 'cor' (English 'kor', not American 'kar') and see if you can reproduce this vowel-sound in the note you are playing. Drop the jaw and focus the sound into the sinus, like a singer. This will not be possible if the reed is too big. Also, experiment by playing the E with very little *vibrato*, almost like a French horn. Discover how 'haunting' the cor anglais can sound. In bar 5, try playing the B with lots of *vibrato*, like a stringed instrument. When a solo is marked *espressivo*, do not simply play with more *vibrato*, but 'say' something: a vowel-sound, a word, a phrase, an idea, a concept. Listen to the harmonies, and they will tell you what to do. Perhaps there is more the student can accomplish then ever he or she had realised. Having planted the idea, they can re-apply it to real pieces of music. I have added some low notes at the end of the piece because these too have a very special character. Low D particularly is a very focused note on the cor. Perhaps that is why it so hard to play it really quietly. Fortunately we do not always have to do so.

For the cor anglais, *vibrato* is best done by varying the air pressure and maybe the vowel sounds too. This will be unsuccessful if the reed is too hard to blow. You can do *vibrato* with the lips but this changes the pitch of the note and that does not sound good on a cor anglais. A really attractive *vibrato* is difficult, and probably different for oboe and cor. It is a fine theory to match cor anglais style to that of oboe playing but in practice the result can be a muddle. The cor anglais is a solo instrument in its own right and you are more likely to play it well if you specialise. Many cor anglais players have to play the oboe as well, in which case it is sensible to think of the two instruments as being different, both in style and in technique.

As a cor anglais player, the only other problem you will have to cope with is ... the envy of those who play other instruments!

Postscript

To be a performer we need: -

1.) To know the pieces very well.

2.) To be able to cope with unfavourable conditions.

3.) To learn to breathe properly not only during a solo, but also just before we play.

4.) To have a reliable technique and to be able to produce a variety of styles and sounds in all registers.

5.) To have sensitivity to the changing musical environment and the ability to adapt.

6.) To draw together the threads of our own perception with those of other people, so that Art is a shared experience.

7.) To have a clear idea of what we are trying to achieve artistically.

8.) A reliable and accurate reflection of the quality of our work.

> Beyond that, **success** in the way we play is a matter of **sheer determination**.

No Air on the A string

Text p. 50

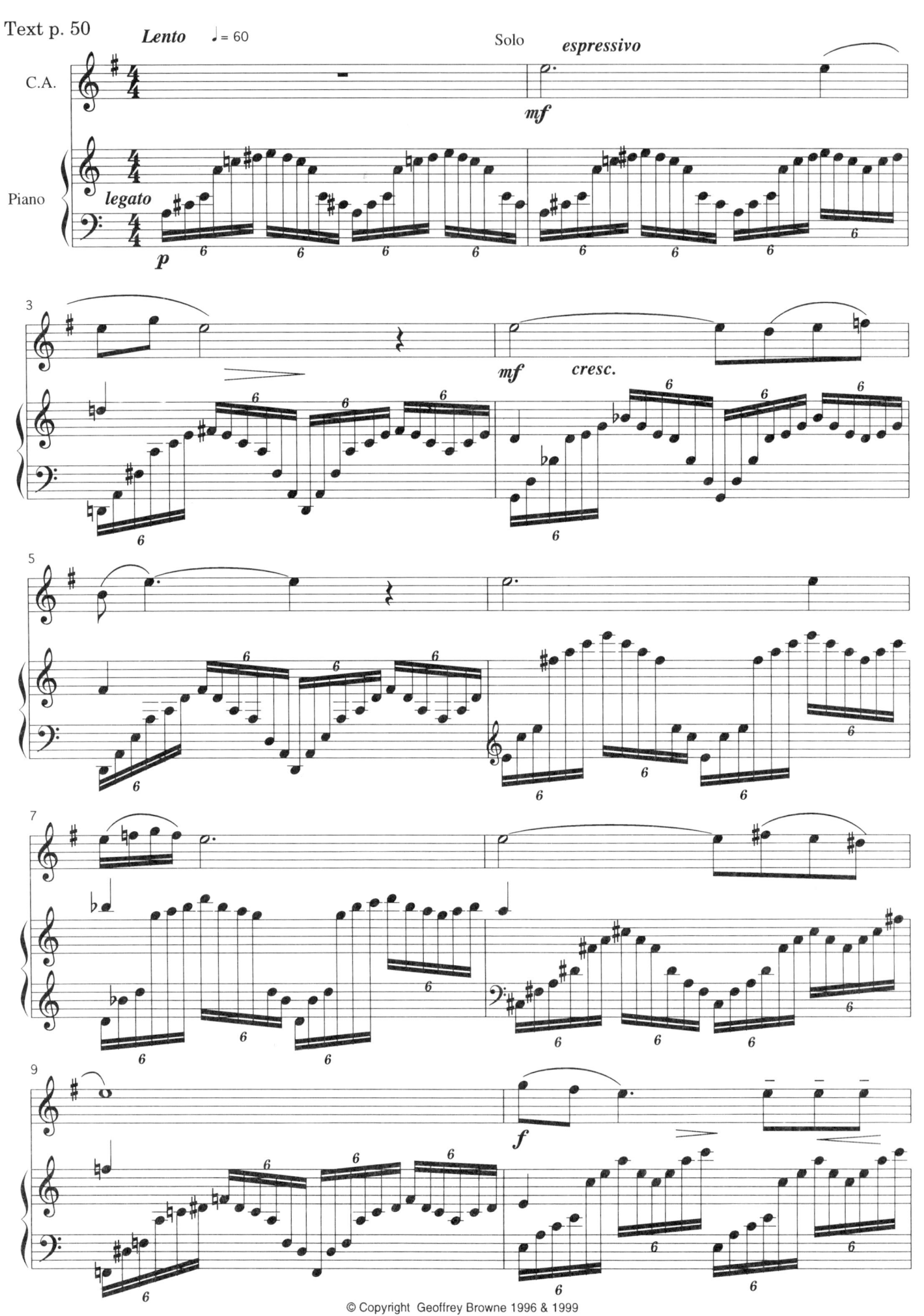

Glossary

Some words and expressions used by Richard Strauss and by Mahler.

allmählich	gradually
anmutig	gracefully
ausbreitend	spread out, extended (like the wings of a bird)
äußerst langsam und zurückhaltend	extremely slow and held back
bedächtig	deliberate
bedeutend langsamer	a lot slower
behaglich	comfortable
belebend	livening up
bewegt	moved; can also mean animated.
breit	broad (not bright!)
drängend	pushed
ermattend	growing weary
etwas	somewhat
gemächlich	leisurely, gentle
gesungen	sung, or chanted
grell	shrill
hervortretend	played out like a solo (similar to 'en dehors') It should stand out from the background even if played by more than one instrument.
immer	always
innig	fervent, inward
klagend	lamentingly
langsam / schnell	slow / quick
leidenschaftlich	passionately
mäßig	moderate
mit Steigerung	with intensification
ohne Nachschläge	no twiddles at the end of the trill
ruhig / ruhiger	calm / calmer
Schalltrichter auf / Schalltrichter in der Höhe	Bells up! (this is ineffective with a cor anglais) 'Schalltrichter' literally means 'sound funnel' or 'bell of an instrument'
scharf	sharply
schwer und dumpf	heavy and dull (used in *Kindertotenlieder*)
schwungvoll	with zest
sehr zart u. geheimnisvoll bis zum Schluß	very sweet and mysterious up till the end (used in Mahler's 4th Symphony)
streng im Takt	strictly in time
Vorschläge	grace notes
wieder	again, once more
zögernd	hesitatingly
zurückhaltend	held back